STACK A NEW DECK

More Great Quilts in 4 Easy Steps

Karla Alexander

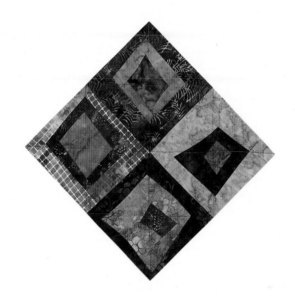

Martingale®
& COMPANY

That Patchwork Place® is an
imprint of Martingale & Company®.

Martingale & Company
20205 144th Avenue NE
Woodinville, WA 98072-8478
www.martingale-pub.com

Printed in China
09 08 07 06 05 04   8 7 6 5 4 3 2

Library of Congress Cataloging-in-Publication Data
Alexander, Karla.
    Stack a new deck : more great quilts in 4 easy steps / Karla Alexander.
        p. cm.
    ISBN 1-56477-537-2
    1. Patchwork—Patterns. 2. Crazy quilts. 3. Rotary cutting.
I. Title.
    TT835 .A43497 2004
    746.46'041—dc22
                                2003027544

Mission Statement

*Dedicated to providing quality products
and service to inspire creativity.*

Credits

PRESIDENT	*Nancy J. Martin*
CEO	*Daniel J. Martin*
PUBLISHER	*Jane Hamada*
EDITORIAL DIRECTOR	*Mary V. Green*
MANAGING EDITOR	*Tina Cook*
TECHNICAL EDITOR	*Ellen Pahl*
COPY EDITOR	*Erana Bumbardatore*
DESIGN DIRECTOR	*Stan Green*
ILLUSTRATOR	*Robin Strobel*
COVER DESIGNER	*Regina Girard*
TEXT DESIGNER	*Trina Stahl*
PHOTOGRAPHER	*Brent Kane*

Dedication

To my mother, LaRue Wilcox.

Acknowledgments

I WOULD LIKE to acknowledge the following people and extend my sincere thanks to each and every one of them.

My profound appreciation and thanks go to my husband, Don, for his continued support. His contributions to this book were enormous.

Joanna Price, for bringing her great enthusiasm, support, laughs, and coffee deliveries to the sewing studio. I treasure our friendship.

Special thanks to my sister, Ruth Hargrave, who showed up at my doorstep and helped with sewing, child care, and cooking in order to help me meet my deadline.

Anne Alexander, my mother-in-law, for being so available and helpful.

Sally Blankenship and Jan Schable for help with hand stitching and endless offers of assistance. Thanks for always believing in me.

SueAnne Suderman for adding her awesome artistic flair while long-arm quilting the quilts "Crazy Curvy Patchwork" and "Funky Curvy Rail."

Sylvia Dorney, owner of Greenbaum's Quilted Forest, generously contributed fabric for several of the projects in this book.

Thanks to my editor, Ellen Pahl, for her guidance through this process, and to the staff at Martingale & Company for their efforts in helping me pursue the creation of my dreams.

Marcus Brothers Fabrics supplied a wonderful selection of bright fabrics for use in the quilt "Hopscotch."

Viking Sewing Machines deserves special thanks for providing me the luxury of the incredible Designer 1.

CONTENTS

Introduction • 6
Getting Started • 8
Making the Crazy Blocks • 10
Quiltmaking Basics • 17

QUILT PROJECTS

INTRODUCTION

M Y PASSION FOR Crazy quilts continues. This book is the result of exploring the never-ending possibilities of the Stack the Deck process presented in my first book, *Stack the Deck! Crazy Quilts in 4 Easy Steps*. From that starting point, quilts have blossomed out of every nook and cranny. Ideas for new quilts mushroom overnight, and I can't keep up with them!

As a quilter and a teacher I love learning new skills, stretching the old ones, and challenging the tough ones. In the process of teaching Stack the Deck methods, I stretched, twisted, and curved the stack technique, soon realizing it would be "crazy" to let it end there. Continue the creative flow with me by stepping out of the traditional quilter's box and taking a crack at a whole new style of quiltmaking. You'll have incredible blocks and designs ready to set into quilt tops in no time at all. Stack fabric squares (or rectangles) into "decks" and slice them into wonderful shapes, curved or straight. Then shuffle the pieces and sew them back together again. Stacking the deck is an opportunity to have fun, be creative, and stitch up a set of unique blocks with an exciting variety of fabrics and unusual shapes.

The Stack the Deck process begins with cutting a square or a rectangle. No difficult little triangles or circles to cut, just squares, squares, and more squares! And what could be easier to cut than a square? Once the squares are cut, you'll stack them into decks, slice them, and then follow a systematic shuffling process—changing the color placement in each block. Then, following the designs in this book, you'll stitch the pieces into incredible blocks.

The Game

HERE ARE THE basic rules for stacking the deck.

1. **Stack** large squares or rectangles of assorted fabrics into a deck, like playing cards.

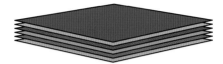

Stack the required number
of fabric squares.

2. **Slice** the deck into shapes following the cutting and sewing guide for your chosen project.

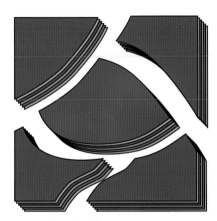

Slice the deck into segments.

3. **Shuffle** the pieces in each stack. (See pages 13–14 for specific shuffling details.)

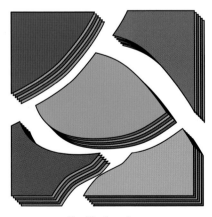

Shuffle the pieces.

4. **Chain-piece** the pieces in each layer of the deck together to make the Crazy blocks. Trim the blocks to the required size.

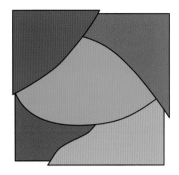

Sew the pieces together.

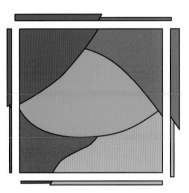

Trim the block to the required size.

It's fast, fun, and easy! Consider this your personal invitation to join me in the game, and we'll go a little crazy together!

Karla Alexander

GETTING STARTED

Select the quilt you want to make first, and refer to the specific fabric requirements and color suggestions for the project. You'll need a wide assortment of cotton fabrics for the quilts in this book.

Choosing Fabrics

An easy way to begin is to use a planned color scheme or focus around a theme such as batiks, florals, or bright juvenile prints. Once you have chosen the theme or look of your quilt, select fabrics that have good contrast with each other. You can use many different fabrics in one quilt top for a scrappy look or, in most projects, you can use the same two or three fabrics throughout your quilt. For example, a quilt requiring ⅜ yard each of four different yellow prints could be easily modified to use 1½ yards of the same yellow fabric for a less scrappy quilt. Refer to the pattern requirements, and keep in mind that most of the photographed quilts feature a wide variety of fabrics. I love to use lots of fabrics, because it gives me the opportunity to use up scraps from my fabric stash. Plus, I am partial to scrappy quilts.

When selecting fabrics, use my 10-Foot Rule, which my students find helpful. Try it and I'm sure you'll find it easy to pick great combinations for your quilts.

Each project lists the fabrics and yardages needed to make a quilt similar to the one in the photograph. I've included Fabric Tips with each project to help you in making your choices. Go through your stash and challenge yourself to use up your leftovers. Cut your squares to the specified size and as long as you do not duplicate the same fabric in a deck, you can use as many fabrics as you please. Remember to have contrast between fabrics, because after they are shuffled most fabrics will end up next to each other somewhere in the quilt.

Ace It!

One of my favorite tools for previewing fabrics is a simple door peephole, available at any home-improvement center. Looking through a peephole will distance you from your choices and help you determine if you have a jumper (a fabric that jumps out at you) or too many fabrics that blend together.

The 10-Foot Rule

STACK THE BOLTS of fabric one on top of another on the counter or stand them side by side. If you're working with your stash, fold and stack the fabrics on a table and fan them out. Then back up approximately 10 feet and take a look. Do the fabrics have good contrast from one another? Does one fabric jump out from the rest? If so, it may need a similar companion. For example, if you have just one red fabric in the mix and your eye goes right to it every time you look at the stack, try adding one or two more reds to the mix for a better balance.

On the other hand, if you have three fabrics from the same color group, back up 10 feet to determine if they appear to blend together, looking like one piece of fabric. Instead of having three medium blues that all muddle together, swap one for a brighter blue, a blue that has another color in the print, or something to liven up the group. Or if you have three greens that don't seem too exciting, swap in some lime, chartreuse, or sage for a peppier mix.

MAKING THE CRAZY BLOCKS

ONCE YOU'VE CHOSEN your fabric, it's time for fun. There are many different styles of blocks used in the projects. Follow the project directions; they'll tell you how many stacks of fabric you need and what square size to start with. The squares are cut a little differently for each project and each type of block. Some blocks are pieced sequentially, as shown in the project's block cutting and sewing guide (see pages 11–12 for details); others are pieced in sections before being reassembled. The cutting and piecing orders are given with each project. Now, begin by stacking the deck.

Red: cutting order   Blue: sewing order

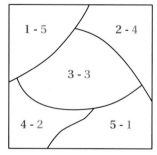 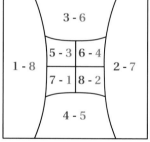 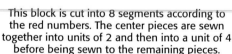

This block is cut into 5 segments according to the red numbers and is sewn back together sequentially following the sewing order in blue.

This block is cut into 8 segments according to the red numbers. The center pieces are sewn together into units of 2 and then into a unit of 4 before being sewn to the remaining pieces.

Stacking the Deck

CUT THE REQUIRED number of squares or rectangles, and stack them up for rotary cutting. When stacking, alternate values in the stack as directed in the specific quilt instructions. Make sure you haven't duplicated a fabric in any one stack (unless project directions specify otherwise). Also keep in mind that the top fabric will eventually be rotated to the bottom of the stack, so make sure the top and bottom fabrics contrast, too. These are scrappy quilts and eventually the identical fabric may end up side by side, but you can keep the blending to a minimum by stacking your cutting decks this way. Some quilts have a controlled deck order with specific fabrics in a specific order.

Slicing the Deck

NOW THAT YOUR decks are all stacked and ready to go, you have two options for cutting them into segments. One option is to cut free form, using your rotary cutter and ruler, and refer to the block cutting and sewing guide, the small-scale version of the block that's included with the project instructions. The other option is to make a full-size cutting guide out of paper to place over the decks as cutting guidelines. You will need to make a paper template for each deck using the block cutting and sewing guide.

Cutting Curves

When cutting curves—with or without a paper template—always use your ruler by gently sliding it along the edge of the curve as you cut. Go very slowly until you get the hang of it. The ruler will ensure that you do not accidentally cut too far into your segments and will help hold the layers in place.

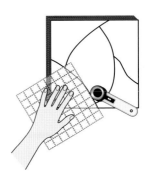

The Block Cutting and Sewing Guide

EACH PROJECT HAS a "block cutting and sewing guide" illustration. It's a reduced version of the block. It gives you the size to cut the original square or rectangle. The cutting order for slicing the stacked decks is given numerically in red on the block segments. The sewing order is listed numerically in blue following the cutting number.

Use the red numbers as your guide when cutting the deck of stacked fabric into segments. Use the blue numbers as the order in which you shuffle and sew the pieces back together. When shuffling, the instructions will refer to the stacks of segments by their blue numbers.

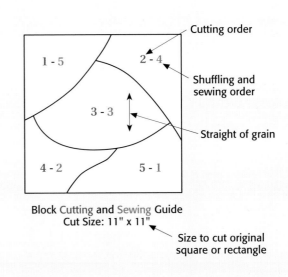

Block Cutting and Sewing Guide
Cut Size: 11" x 11"

FREE-FORM CUTTING

Cutting free form allows you to skip the step of making a paper template for each deck of fabric. Refer to the block cutting and sewing guide for the project that you have chosen, use a chalk marker, and draw the cutting lines onto the top fabric in the deck. Once you're satisfied with the lines, lay your rotary-cutting ruler on top of the stacked fabrics and cut your deck apart on the chalk lines. Make the first cut as indicated in the block drawing. Keeping the stack together, shift the ruler to make the next cut. Continue cutting apart the pieces, referring to the block drawing.

Now you're ready to shuffle the deck as described in "Shuffling Basics" on pages 13–14.

Ace It!

You may move the cut stacks out of the way a bit, but keep the stacks of segments in the same position as they are in the block cutting and sewing guide. This will help keep the stacks in the correct order.

CUTTING WITH PAPER TEMPLATES

For this method, you will need clean newsprint paper, freezer paper, or wrapping paper (use the unprinted side).

1. Refer to the block cutting and sewing guide for the project you have chosen. Draw a square or rectangle the same size as your cut fabric on a piece of paper; then draw the cutting lines. It's not critical to have exact measurements for the segments. Go by what you like. When you're happy with your template drawing, make as many copies of it as there are fabric decks in the project.

2. Cut the templates out around the outer edges of the square or rectangle.

3. Place the paper template on top of your fabric stack. Pin the pattern to the stack, pinning through each numbered segment to secure it. Flat-head flower pins work great for this task because you'll be putting your acrylic ruler over them for cutting.

4. Use your rotary cutter and ruler to slice through the paper and all layers of fabric on every drawn line.

5. Remove the pins and the paper template. Reassemble the template (like a jigsaw puzzle) to the side of the cut blocks as a reference. Now you're ready to shuffle the deck as described in "Shuffling Basics."

Variety—the Spice of Crazy Blocks

ONCE YOU GET the hang of cutting your decks, try varying the angles from one stack to another. You can do this with free-form cutting or with your template by altering the lines slightly. This adds more variety and interest to your finished quilt. Most of the quilts in this book were made using a specific template; however, with each new deck I slightly changed the lines and angles.

Another way to add variety is to add more segments to a block template. Keep in mind that this requires more cuts and more seams, which means the finished blocks will be smaller than ones with fewer cuts and seams.

Shuffling Basics

THERE ARE TWO different shuffling methods used in this book: the traditional shuffle and the controlled shuffle. The instructions for each quilt project specify which method to use.

TRADITIONAL SHUFFLING

Traditional shuffling is always the same process, regardless of how many segments there are in your particular block. Whether you have three segments or eight segments in your block, you shuffle each stack just once. When shuffling, use the blue numbers. The shuffling order is the same as the sewing order.

1. Take the top layer off the segment 1 stack and place it on the bottom of the stack.

2. Take two layers of fabric off the segment 2 stack and place them on the bottom of that stack.

3. Take three layers of fabric off the segment 3 stack and place them on the bottom of that stack.

4. Continue shuffling each stack, removing the same number of fabrics from the top as the number of the segment you're shuffling, until all the stacks have been shuffled. If the number of fabric layers is equal to the number of cut segments, the last stack in each block will not be shuffled. For instance, if you have a stack of five squares and you are cutting a five-segment block, you need only shuffle the first four segments because the last set is already in place.

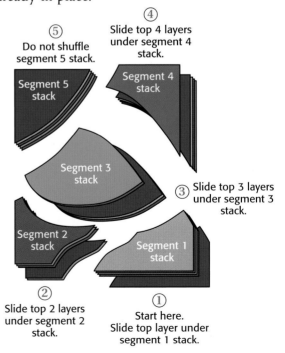

⑤ Do not shuffle segment 5 stack.

④ Slide top 4 layers under segment 4 stack.

③ Slide top 3 layers under segment 3 stack.

② Slide top 2 layers under segment 2 stack.

① Start here. Slide top layer under segment 1 stack.

Segment 5 stack

Segment 4 stack

Segment 3 stack

Segment 2 stack

Segment 1 stack

CONTROLLED SHUFFLING

Controlled shuffling involves specific segments of the block. Certain segments are shuffled a given number of times. For example, some blocks appear to have a square in a square. Shuffling just the center square once results in outer fabric strips that all remain the same. Place the top center square on the bottom of the stack.

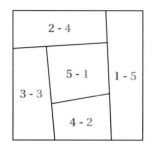

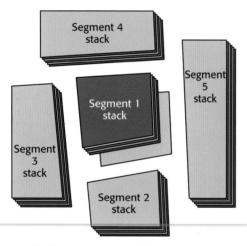

Shuffle segment 1 by sliding top layer under the stack. The remaining pieces stay in place.

Paper Layout

ONCE THE SHUFFLING process is complete, regardless of which method was used, reassemble and pin each stack of segments to a piece of paper. Be sure to pin through all layers. Keep them in the exact order and layout in which they were shuffled. The pins will keep the segments in order; I also add a safety pin to the top layer of stack 1. This helps to keep the pieces in the correct order when sewing (chain-piecing) the segments together. Once the segments are secure, use a pen-

cil and trace along the cutting lines onto the paper. The lines will create a handy reference so that you can keep all the pieces in order and sew them together correctly.

Sewing the Blocks

TO DETERMINE WHERE to begin sewing first, number the segments following the order given in blue in the block cutting and sewing guide for the project you're making. For most blocks, sewing order is the exact opposite of the cutting order. For instance, the last segment sliced will be segment 1 for sewing. The next to the last piece is segment 2. The segment cut before that will be segment 3, the one before that will be segment 4, and so on. The very first segment cut will be the last sewn and have the highest number. Once you have determined the sewing order, use a pencil and note the number on the paper, next to the appropriate stack.

Keep the stacks in their shuffled order while sewing; otherwise you'll end up duplicating a fabric within a block. After chain-piecing all layers of segments 1 and 2 together, layer 1 always needs to be returned to the top of the stack, then the second layer, and so on. It's easy to reverse the order while ironing or clipping the pieces apart, so I rely on the safety pin in the top layer of the stack to keep the correct order. When you begin sewing again, you'll automatically know the combined pieces are in the right sequence if the safety pin is on top of the stack. If the pin is not on the top of the stack, this indicates the order was probably reversed and will need to be corrected before continuing. Keep the safety pin in place until all the blocks in the stack have been sewn.

1. Unpin stacks 1 and 2 and peel off the top piece from each. Flip piece 1 onto piece 2 with right sides facing and stitch the pieces together.

2. Pick up the next layer from stacks 1 and 2 and sew them together in the same manner. You can chain-piece the units together as shown, continuing until all the segment 1 and segment 2 pieces are stitched together in pairs.

3. Press the units open, with the seam allowance pressed to one side. Clip them apart, being careful to restack them in their original order.

4. With right sides together, sew segment 3 to the units you just made. Chain-piece the units as before.

5. Press the units open, clip them apart, and restack them in their original order.

6. Continue adding segments in numerical sewing order until all have been added.

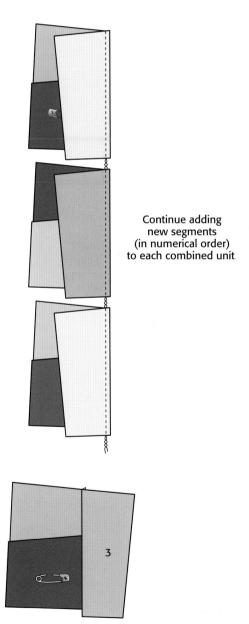

Continue adding
new segments
(in numerical order)
to each combined unit.

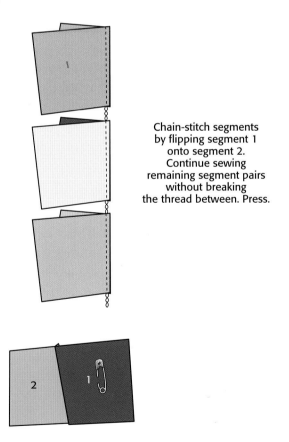

Chain-stitch segments
by flipping segment 1
onto segment 2.
Continue sewing
remaining segment pairs
without breaking
the thread between. Press.

Trimming

DUE TO THE seam allowances, the pieced segments will shrink up and tend to be shorter than the next segment they are being added to. To remedy this, refer to your paper layout and trim the excess fabric as you go to even the edges for the next piece. Return to the paper layout and continue chain-piecing (be sure to maintain the original sewing order).

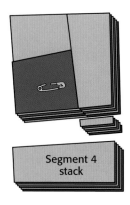

Move the pieced segments and the next group of segments to be sewn onto your cutting mat. Trim excess off the lower edge of the stack, through all layers. Keep the cut at the same angle and curve of the excess edge.

Segment 4 stack

When all the pieces are sewn together, lay a square rotary-cutting ruler on top of the finished blocks and trim to the size specified in the pattern instructions.

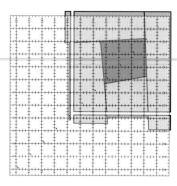

Sewing Curves

MANY OF THE quilts in this book have slight curves. When marking the cutting lines, add hatch marks along the diagonal of the square with a chalk pencil *before* shuffling. Carefully pick up the unshuffled segments and use a sharp pair of scissors to make snips, about ⅛" deep, through all layers at the marks. The snips are easily matched when sewing. Take care that you don't snip too far into the seam allowance. Pin together at this point, if desired, to keep the pieces aligned for sewing.

Another way to mark the centers of the lower layers is to carefully pick up the unshuffled segments and fold the segments on the marked line. Use an iron to gently press a crease to use for matching. Keep in mind that the blocks will be uneven and will be trimmed after sewing, so precise matching of curves is not essential.

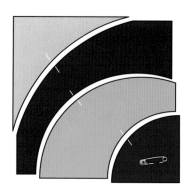

To easily piece the curves with minimal pinning or clipping, make a guide on the bed of your sewing machine. Use a strip of mounting tape as described in "Tools and Supplies" on page 17. Cut off a small strip, approximately 1" to 2" long. Leave the thin, protective top layer on the tape and press the sticky side in place ¼" from the needle, extending in front of the presser foot. Gently align the curved edges, approximately 1" to 2" in front of the needle and up against the edge of the mounting tape as you sew. Since the blocks will be trimmed to size later, you don't have to fuss with matching the bottom edges!

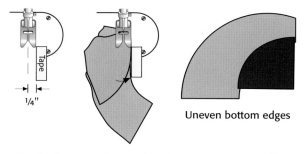

Tape

¼"

Uneven bottom edges

Gently align raw edges against the tape as you sew. Align only a short section, and don't match the bottom edges.

QUILTMAKING BASICS

HERE IS A rundown of the basic tools and techniques you'll need to make any of the quilts in this book. A sewing machine in good working order, high-quality supplies and tools, accuracy, and a whole lot of passion are the ingredients in my recipe for a good quilting experience. Refer back to this section as needed when you're making your quilt project.

Tools and Supplies

THE FOLLOWING TOOLS will make your Crazy quilt experience both fun and easy.

Rotary cutter: Choose a medium to large rotary cutter. Start with a sharp new blade that will allow you to cut through several layers of fabric at a time.

Cutting mat: A mat that is 17" x 23" should be sufficient for cutting blocks and borders. You might want to use one side for cutting curves and the other side for straight cuts.

Acrylic rulers: A 6" x 24" ruler is great for cutting fabric into strips. A square ruler is essential for cutting squares and trimming up pieced blocks. A 12½" x 12½" square is best, but depending on your project, a 6" x 6" or other smaller square ruler may be adequate.

Mounting tape: I use this as a guide when sewing curved pieces. This is a double-sticky tape with foam backing that comes on a roll. Mounting tape can be purchased at most hardware stores.

Sewing thread: Use good-quality, 100%-cotton thread for piecing. Match the thread to the general value of the fabrics, but in most cases you can use neutral colors: light, medium, and dark values of tan and gray.

Quilting thread: Choosing your quilting thread is usually one of the last decisions to be made, but it is one of my favorite steps! I use a variety of thread from 100% cotton to silky rayons and metallics. Have fun choosing your thread and always buy the best you can afford; it will pay off in the end.

Seam ripper: Keep a seam ripper handy for easy stitch removal.

Sewing machine: Be sure your sewing machine is in good working order and sews a reliable and balanced straight stitch. If you plan on machine quilting, you will need a walking foot and possibly a darning foot depending on the style of quilting you choose.

Basting spray (optional): Spray basting is a time-saver when layering the quilt sandwich for machine quilting. Do not use it for hand quilting.

Assembling the Quilt Top

ONCE YOUR BLOCKS are made, arrange them following the illustration or directions provided with each quilt. Play with the blocks, twisting, turning, and substituting them until you're satisfied with the arrangement. I try to separate identical prints so that they are not next to each other. In some patterns, you'll have extra blocks to choose from. When you're happy with the arrangement, you can use any extra blocks to stitch up a coordinating pillow, or attach a label to one and stitch it to the back of your quilt.

Join the blocks in horizontal rows, matching the seams between the blocks. Press seams in the opposite direction from row to row so opposing seams will butt against each other, or follow the pressing arrows in the quilt diagrams. For quilts with sashing strips, follow the illustration or directions provided with each quilt to arrange the blocks and sashing strips. Join the blocks and horizontal sashing strips into rows, and press seams toward the sashing strips. Join the rows of blocks and vertical sashing strips.

Adding Borders

1. Refer to the cutting directions for each quilt project and cut the required number of strips for the border.

2. Remove the selvages and sew the border strips together to make one long strip. Press the seams to one side.

A Note about Materials and Cutting

ALL YARDAGES ARE based on 42"-wide fabrics, with 40" of usable width after preshrinking. When following the cutting instructions, cut all strips across the fabric width (cross grain).

3. Measure the length of the quilt top through the center. Cut two border strips to that measurement. Mark the center of the quilt edges and the border strips.

4. Pin the borders to opposite sides of the quilt, matching the center marks and ends. Sew the borders in place, easing in any fullness.

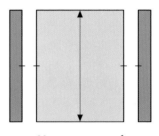

Measure center of
quilt, top to bottom.
Mark centers.

5. Measure the width of the quilt top through the center, including the side borders just added. Cut two border strips to that measurement. Mark, pin, and sew the borders in place as described for the side borders. Press the seams toward the border.

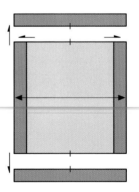

Measure center of quilt,
side to side, including borders.
Mark centers.

Fusible-Web Appliqué

SEVERAL OF THE projects in this book include designs using fusible-web appliqué. The paper-backed fusible web is sold in both heavy and lightweight types. I used the lightweight fusible web and added a machine buttonhole stitch, a straight stitch, a satin stitch, or a zigzag stitch over the raw edges. For appliqués that won't be stitched around, use a heavier-weight fusible web.

1. Trace each part of the selected appliqué design onto the paper side of the fusible web. The patterns are given in mirror image because the fusible web shape is applied to the wrong side of the fabric. When finished, it will be the same image as in the completed quilt.

2. Cut loosely around the traced designs on the fusible web. Do not cut on the tracing lines at this point.

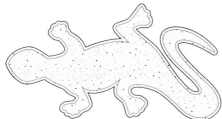

Fusible Appliqué Shape

3. Position each piece of fusible web on the wrong side of selected fabrics and press, following the manufacturer's directions. Cut out each shape on the drawn lines. Remove the paper backing.

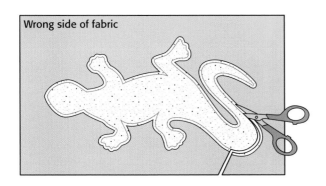

Wrong side of fabric

4. Arrange the shapes in the desired position on the right side of the background fabric. Fuse in place according to the manufacturer's directions.

5. Sew around the edges of the appliqué shape, using the stitch you desire.

Layering and Basting

1. Prepare the backing according to directions for each individual project.

2. Lay out the backing, wrong side up, on a large table. Use masking tape to hold it in place, being careful not to stretch the backing too tight but just enough to keep it nice and smooth. If you don't have a large table, move to the floor and use T-pins inserted into the carpet.

3. Lay out the batting on top of the backing. The backing and batting should be at least 2" to 3" larger all around than the quilt top. Smooth out any wrinkles.

4. Center and lay the pieced top on the batting, right side up. Make sure that the quilt top is "square" with the backing.

5. Baste the layers together, using one of the three techniques that follow. (My personal favorite is spray basting.)

Backing Seams

When piecing your backing, press the seams to one side for a stronger seam. If you will be hand quilting, however, press them open to reduce bulk.

HAND BASTING

Basting by hand is recommended if you will be hand quilting.

1. Use a large needle and a long length of thread. Begin in the center of the quilt and baste diagonally with large stitches to each corner.

2. Baste horizontal and vertical rows across the quilt top, each approximately 6" apart. Finish with a basting stitch around all four sides.

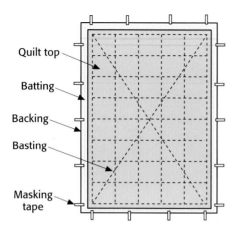

PIN BASTING

Use pin basting if you plan to do machine quilting. Pin basting is most easily done if you have a large table to lay the quilt on. Use 1" safety pins, and pin every 5" to 6" across the quilt top, beginning in the center and working out. Place the pins where they will not interfere with your planned quilting stitches.

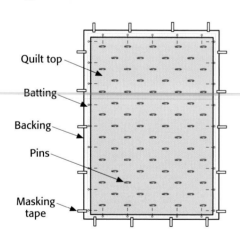

SPRAY BASTING

Spray basting is relatively new and works great on cotton and cotton-blend battings. A few things to keep in mind for successful spray basting: First, make sure you work in a well-ventilated area. Second, use a large sheet under your quilt to catch

any overspray. Third, make doubly sure that the backing is anchored down without any wrinkles!

1. Arrange the backing, batting, and quilt top on a large sheet.

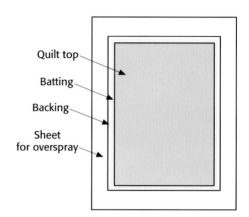

2. Fold the quilt top back, horizontally, about a quarter of the way down; fold down again so that half of the quilt top is folded back on itself in quarters, and the batting is exposed.

3. Repeat with the batting, folding it back in quarters, exposing the upper half of the backing.

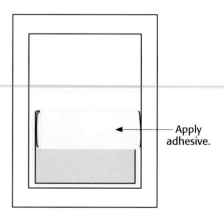

4. Lightly spray the back of the exposed quarter of batting. Gently replace it on the backing. Slide the can of basting spray along the top of the sprayed batting to smooth out any wrinkles. Lightly spray the back of the remaining quarter of exposed batting, carefully replacing it on the backing and smoothing out any wrinkles.

5. Lightly spray a quarter of the front of the exposed batting, not the quilt top, and replace a quarter of the exposed quilt top onto the batting. Smooth out any wrinkles. Repeat for the remaining quarter.

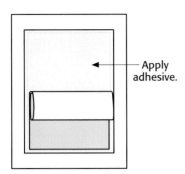

Apply adhesive.

6. Once one end is completed, repeat the above steps for the opposite end, always working in quarters. When finished, remove the tape or T-pins and turn the basted quilt over. Carefully smooth out any wrinkles.

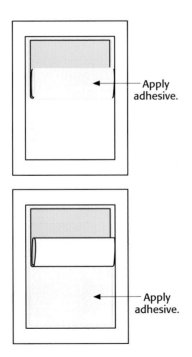

Apply adhesive.

Apply adhesive.

Binding

BINDING FINISHES THE edges of your quilt. I prefer a double-fold, straight-grain binding, often referred to as a "French fold" binding. I often choose one of the prints used in the quilt for the binding, but sometimes I introduce a new fabric. Since I frequently use busy prints in my quilts, I might choose a coordinating print that reads as a solid from a distance.

1. Trim the batting and backing even with the quilt top.

2. Refer to the cutting list for each individual project and cut the required number of strips for binding.

3. Remove selvages and join binding strips right sides together as shown, making one long piece of binding. Trim the excess fabric and press the seam allowances open to reduce bulk.

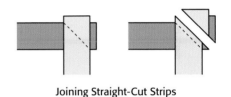

Joining Straight-Cut Strips

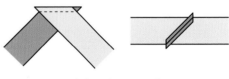

Joining Bias-Cut Strips

4. Fold the strip in half lengthwise, wrong sides together, and press.

5. Lay the binding on the front of the quilt, aligning raw edges. Begin about 10" to 18" away from a corner and leave a 10" tail. Use a ¼" seam allowance and a walking foot to sew the binding to the front of your quilt. Stop sewing ¼" from the corner and carefully backstitch two to three stitches. Clip the thread and remove the quilt from the machine.

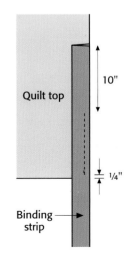

10"

Quilt top

¼"

Binding strip

6. Rotate the quilt so you can sew down the next side. Fold the binding up, creating a 45° angle, and then back down, even with the second side of the quilt. A little pleat will form at the corner.

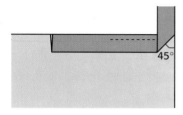

7. Start stitching at the folded edge. Continue stitching the binding to the quilt, stopping at the corners until you're approximately 10" from the starting point. Remove the quilt from the sewing machine.

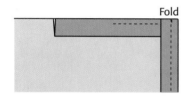

8. Fold back the beginning and end binding strips, so they meet together in the center of the unsewn portion of the quilt edge. Finger-press the folded edges.

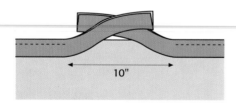

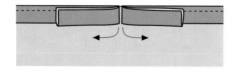

9. Unfold both ends of the binding and match the center points of the two finger-pressed folds together, forming an X as shown. Pin and sew the two ends together on the diagonal of the fold lines. Trim the excess binding ¼" from the seam. Finger-press the new seam allowance

open and fold the binding back in half. Finish sewing the binding to the quilt edge.

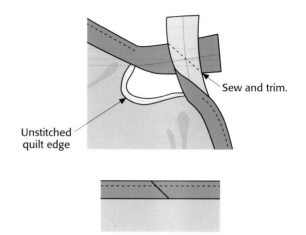

10. Fold the binding over the quilt edge and around to the back side. With the folded edge covering the machine stitching, hand sew the binding in place, mitering the corners as you go.

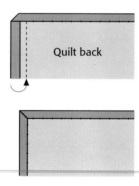

Labeling Your Quilt

FINISH YOUR QUILT by adding a label to the back. The label should, at a minimum, contain your name and date. Add other information as desired: the name of the quilt, your hometown, who the quilt was made for, what the occasion was, and so on. Use a permanent fabric marker to write the information on a piece of fabric and then hand sew it to the back of your quilt. To make it easier to write on fabric, press a piece of freezer paper onto the wrong side of the fabric. Remove the freezer paper before sewing the label to the quilt.

BENT OUT OF SQUARE

Made entirely out of batiks, this quilt offers you the opportunity to shuffle a wide variety of colors and try your hand at free-form cutting "bent" squares.

FINISHED QUILT: 60" x 78½" • FINISHED BLOCK: 6½" x 6½"

This dramatic quilt allows you to enjoy a large assortment of batiks all in one quilt. Each of the "bent" squares is different, creating windows of luscious colors that entice your eyes to roam from block to block.

Materials

Yardage is based on 42"-wide fabric.

- 1 yard of purple batik for outer border
- ⅝ yard of fuchsia batik for inner border
- ⅜ yard each of 8 different medium to dark batiks for blocks
- ⅜ yard each of 8 different medium to light batiks for blocks
- ⅜ yard of gold batik for middle border
- ¼ yard each of 4 different medium to dark batiks for side setting triangles
- 4⅝ yards of fabric for backing
- ¾ yard of purple for binding
- 64" x 83" piece of batting

Fabric Tips

Take advantage of all those glorious batiks. The goal is to have a large selection of contrasting prints. Begin by choosing several favorites, lay them side by side, and then start adding contrasting colors. Stand back and take a look, adding and subtracting prints until you're satisfied with your selections.

Cutting

All measurements include ¼" seam allowances.

From each of the 8 medium to dark batiks, cut:

- 1 strip, 9¾" x 42"; crosscut each strip into 4 squares, 9¾" x 9¾", for a total of 32 squares. You will have 2 extra squares; use these for the corner setting triangles.

From the two leftover 9¾" squares, cut:

- 2 squares, 6" x 6". Cut the squares in half diagonally to yield 4 half-square triangles.★

★*Note that the corner setting triangles are cut slightly oversized to allow for trimming and squaring up the quilt top.*

From each of the 8 medium to light batiks, cut:

- 1 strip, 9¾" x 42"; crosscut each strip into 4 squares, 9¾" x 9¾", for a total of 32 squares. You will have 2 extra squares.

From each of the 4 medium to dark batiks, cut:

- 1 strip, 6" x 42"

From the fuchsia batik, cut:

- 6 strips, 2½" x 42"

From the gold batik, cut:

- 7 strips, 1½" x 42"

From the purple batik, cut:

- 7 strips, 4½" x 42"

From the binding fabric, cut:

- 8 strips, 2½" x 42"

Making the Blocks

REFER TO "Making the Crazy Blocks" on pages 10–16 as needed.

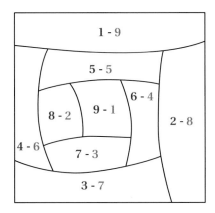

Block Cutting and Sewing Guide
Cut Size: 9¾" x 9¾"

1. Arrange the 60 squares into 10 decks of six each, alternating dark with light. Each deck should contain six different prints. Secure the decks with a pin through all layers until ready to sew.

2. Referring to the block cutting and sewing guide and the cutting variations, slice the decks.

3. Referring to the shuffling guide, shuffle the decks. You will shuffle the center piece under one time, and the surrounding four strips two times each. The remaining outside strips are not shuffled; this creates continuous "rounds" of the same color.

4. Make 60 blocks. Press the seam allowances toward the outside, away from the center. Trim the blocks to 7" x 7". You will have one extra pieced block to use as an option when arranging the blocks.

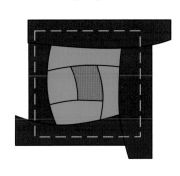
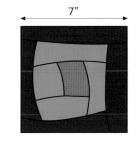

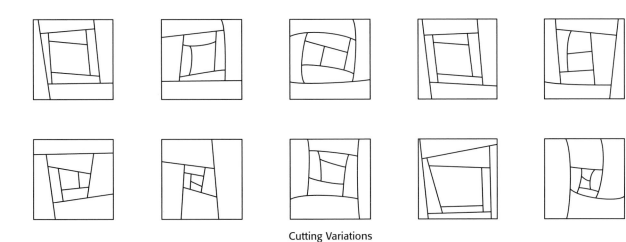

Cutting Variations

Shuffling Guide

USE THE controlled shuffle described on page 14 for the decks in this quilt.

- Remove the top layer of center segment 1 and place on the bottom of the stack.
- Remove the top two layers of inner segments 2, 3, 4, and 5 and place them on the bottom of the stack.
- Do not shuffle the outer segments 6, 7, 8, and 9.

Assembling the Quilt Top

1. Use the 45° line on your rotary-cutting ruler and cut each of the medium to dark batik strips into 5 triangles as shown, for a total of 20 triangles. The triangles are cut slightly oversized to allow for trimming and squaring up the quilt top.

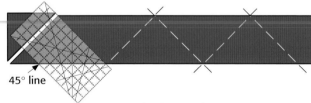

45° line

Cut 5 triangles from each strip.

2. Arrange the side setting triangles and blocks into diagonal rows. Move and turn the blocks until you're satisfied with the arrangement. Try to arrange the blocks so identical prints are not side by side in the finished layout. Look through a door peephole or use the 10-foot rule to check the color and balance.

3. Sew the blocks and side setting triangles together in diagonal rows and press as directed by the arrows. Add the corner setting triangles and press the seams toward the triangles.

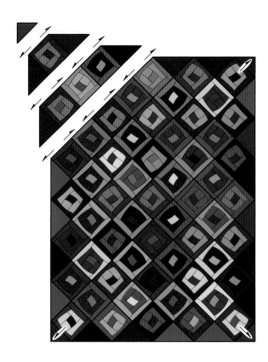

4. Use your rotary cutter and ruler to trim and square up the quilt top. Be sure to allow ¼" seam allowances beyond the points of the blocks.

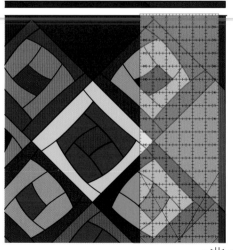

Trim ¼" from block corners.
¼"

5. Refer to "Adding Borders" on page 18. Sew the inner-border strips together to make one long strip. Measure the quilt and cut the inner-border strips to size. Sew them to the sides of the quilt. Measure and add the inner-border strips to the top and bottom. Press the seams toward the border strips. Repeat with the middle and outer borders.

Finishing Your Quilt

REFER TO "Layering and Basting" on pages 19–21 and "Binding" on pages 21–22.

1. Divide the backing fabric crosswise into two panels, each approximately 83" long. Remove the selvages and sew the pieces together along two long edges to make the backing. Press the seam to one side.

2. Layer the quilt top with the batting and backing, with the backing seam parallel to the sides of the quilt. Baste the layers together.

3. Hand or machine quilt as desired. I machine quilted mine with variegated purple, blue, and fuchsia thread, using a straight stitch for the blocks and light stippling for the borders.

4. Trim the backing and batting even with the quilt top and bind the quilt.

SQUARE DANCE

*Pieced from flannels, this cozy quilt is a snap to make. Tilt and turn the cuts
and swing your blocks in all directions to make the "square dance"!*
FINISHED QUILT: 63" x 84" • FINISHED BLOCK: 7" x 7"

With my sons in mind, I made this quilt out of 100% cotton flannel plaids. It's fun; it's easy; it's big. You'll be sewing in the fast lane and making a quilt in practically no time at all!

Materials

Yardage is based on 42"-wide fabric.

- 1½ yards of dark plaid flannel for outer border
- ½ yard of light plaid flannel for inner border
- ⅜ yard *each* of 9 different light flannels for blocks
- ⅜ yard *each* of 9 different medium to dark flannels for blocks
- 5 yards of flannel for backing
- ¾ yard of black flannel for binding
- 67" x 88" piece of batting

Fabric Tips

I made this quilt completely out of flannels, but regular quilting cotton will work just fine. Gather plaids in large and small scales. I combined old and new prints. Be sure to assemble a large selection of contrasting plaids.

Cutting

All measurements include ¼" seam allowances.

From each of the 9 light flannels, cut:
- 1 strip, 9" x 42"; crosscut each strip into 4 squares, 9" x 9", for a total of 36 squares

From each of the 9 medium to dark flannels, cut:
- 1 strip, 9" x 42"; crosscut each strip into 4 squares, 9" x 9", for a total of 36 squares

From the light plaid, cut:
- 7 strips, 2" x 42"

From the dark plaid, cut:
- 8 strips, 6" x 42"

From the binding fabric, cut:
- 8 strips, 2½" x 42"

Making the Blocks

REFER TO "Making the Crazy Blocks" on pages 10–16 as needed.

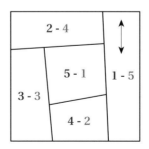 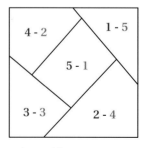

Block Cutting and Sewing Guides
Cut Size: 9" x 9"

1. Arrange the 72 squares into nine decks of 8 each, alternating dark with light. Each deck should contain eight different prints. Secure the decks with a pin through all layers until ready to sew.

Shuffling Guide

USE THE controlled shuffle described on page 14 for the decks in this quilt.

- Remove the top layer of center segment 1 and place on the bottom of the stack.
- Don't shuffle any other segments.

2. Referring to the block cutting and sewing guide, slice the decks. Vary the angles and widths when cutting to change the size and shape of the center piece.

3. Referring to shuffling guide, shuffle the deck.

4. Make 72 blocks. Trim the blocks to 7½" x 7½". You will have 2 extra blocks.

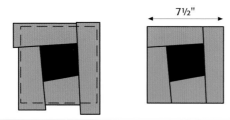

4. Refer to "Adding Borders" on page 18. Sew the seven inner-border strips together to make one long strip. Measure the quilt top and cut the inner-border strips to size. Sew the strips to the sides of the quilt, and then measure and add the top and bottom borders. Press the seams toward the border strips. Repeat with the outer border.

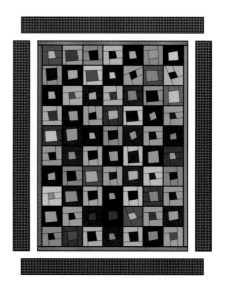

Finishing Your Quilt

REFER TO "Layering and Basting" on pages 19–21 and "Binding" on pages 21–22.

1. Divide the backing fabric crosswise into two panels, each approximately 90" long. Remove the selvages and sew the pieces together along two long edges to make the backing. Press the seam to one side.

2. Layer the quilt top with the batting and backing, with the backing seam parallel to the sides of the quilt. Baste the layers together.

3. Hand or machine quilt as desired. I machine quilted mine using a large stipple pattern through the blocks. For the borders, I stitched in-the-ditch with a straight stitch.

4. Trim the backing and batting even with the quilt top and bind the quilt.

Assembling the Quilt Top

1. Arrange 10 horizontal rows of seven blocks each. Move and turn the blocks until you're satisfied with the arrangement. Try to arrange the blocks so identical prints are not side by side in the finished layout. Look through a door peephole or use the 10-foot rule to check the color and block balance.

2. Sew the blocks together in rows. Press the seams in opposite directions from row to row.

3. Sew the rows together and press the seams in one direction.

GARDEN VIEW

This quilt is truly a garden fantasy, giving you plenty of opportunity to experiment with florals.
FINISHED QUILT: 64½" x 86" • FINISHED BLOCK: 7½" x 7½"

*M*y mother instilled in me a love of flowers at a very early age. She had a wonderful flower garden and always filled our house with fresh bouquets. To this day, I can't resist the awesome view of a garden. I designed this quilt with her in mind.

Materials

Yardage is based on 42"-wide fabric.

- 1⅜ yards of dark purple floral for outer border
- ⅞ yard of medium purple print for side and corner triangles
- ½ yard of light green print for inner border
- ⅜ yard *each* of 9 different light florals for blocks
- ⅜ yard *each* of 9 different dark florals for blocks
- 5¼ yards of fabric for backing
- ¾ yard of purple print for binding
- 70" x 92" piece of batting

Fabric Tips

If you enjoy flower gardens, you'll enjoy the process of selecting fabrics for this quilt. Choose a variety of floral prints, half with a light background and half with a dark background. Choose prints in both small and medium scales, prints with at least three or more colors, and prints with many differently shaped flowers and leaves.

Cutting

All measurements include ¼" seam allowances.

From each of 8 light florals, cut:
- 1 strip, 9 " x 42"; crosscut each strip into 4 squares, 9" x 9", for a total of 32 squares

From the 1 remaining light floral, cut:
- 1 strip, 9" x 42"; crosscut into 3 squares, 9" x 9"

From each of 8 dark florals, cut:
- 1 strip, 9" x 42"; crosscut each strip into 4 squares, 9" x 9", for a total of 32 squares

From the 1 remaining dark floral, cut:
- 1 strip, 9" x 42"; crosscut into 3 squares, 9" x 9"

From the medium purple print, cut:
- 5 squares, 12" x 12"; cut in half diagonally twice to yield 20 side setting triangles
- 2 squares, 6½" x 6½"; cut in half diagonally once to yield 4 corner setting triangles

From the light green print, cut:
- 7 strips, 1¾" x 42"

From the dark purple floral, cut:
- 8 strips, 5" x 42"

From the purple print, cut:
- 8 strips, 2½" x 42"

Shuffling Guide

USE THE controlled shuffle described on page 14 for the decks in this quilt.

- Remove the top layer of center segment 1 and place on the bottom of the stack.
- Do not shuffle any other segments.

Making the Blocks

REFER TO "Making the Crazy Blocks" on pages 10–16 as needed.

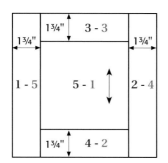

Block Cutting and Sewing Guide
Cut Size: 9" x 9"

1. Arrange the 70 squares into eight decks of 8 each and one deck of 6, alternating dark with light. Each deck should contain eight different prints (or six for the smaller deck). Secure the decks with a pin through all layers.

2. For this block, you will use a controlled cut. Using a ruler and rotary cutter, cut a 1¾" strip off the right and left sides of the deck.

3. Move the cut pieces away and cut a 1¾" strip off the top and bottom of the deck.

4. Referring to the shuffling guide, shuffle the deck .

5. Make 70 blocks. Press seam allowances toward the outside strips, away from the center. Trim the blocks to 8" x 8". You will have 11 extra pieced blocks to use as an option when arranging the blocks. You can use the extra to make a pillow or pillowcase.

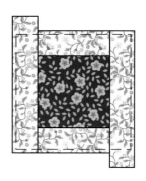
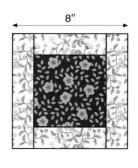

Make a charming pillow from leftover blocks.

Assembling the Quilt Top

1. Arrange the side setting triangles and blocks into diagonal rows, alternating the blocks having light center squares with blocks having dark center squares. Move and turn the blocks until you're satisfied with the arrangement. Try to arrange the blocks so identical prints are not side by side in the finished layout. Look through a door peephole or use the 10-foot rule to check the color and block balance.

2. Sew the blocks and side setting triangles together in diagonal rows and press as directed by the arrows. Add the corner setting triangles last and press the seams toward the triangles.

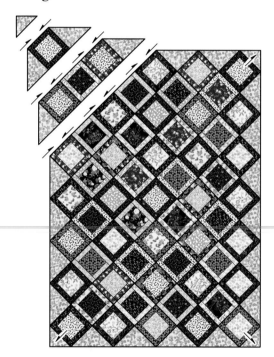

3. Refer to "Adding Borders" on page 18. Sew the inner-border strips together to make one long strip. Measure the length of the quilt top and cut the inner-border strips to size. Sew them to the sides of the quilt. Press the seams toward the border strips. Measure and sew the inner-border strips to the top and bottom. Repeat with the outer border.

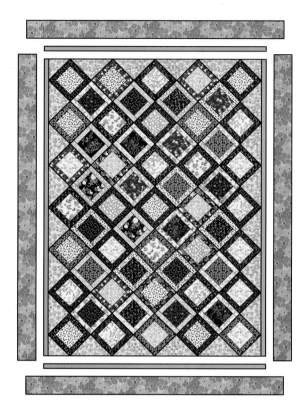

Finishing Your Quilt

Refer to "Layering and Basting" on pages 19–21 and "Binding" on pages 21–22.

1. Divide the backing fabric crosswise into two panels, each approximately 92" long. Remove the selvages and sew the pieces together lengthwise to make the backing. Press the seam to one side.

2. Layer the quilt top with the batting and backing, with the backing seam parallel to the sides of the quilt. Baste the layers together.

3. Hand or machine quilt as desired. I machine quilted mine using a straight, machine-guided stitch horizontally and vertically through the blocks. I also used a straight stitch in the borders.

4. Trim the backing and batting even with the quilt top and bind the quilt.

COTTAGE QUARTERS

Grab a handful of plaids and make up this fast little quilt. To give this quilt an entirely new look, vary the strip widths.
Finished quilt: 48" x 67" • Finished block: 8½" x 8½"

This vibrant quilt can be considered part of the Log Cabin family, only it's easier. The block is somewhat like a half Log Cabin. I used contrasting plaids with a couple of subtle strips thrown in, but any group of contrasting prints would work.

Materials

Yardage is based on 42"-wide fabric.

- 1⅝ yards of pink plaid A for blocks, outer border, and sashing squares
- 1¼ yards of yellow plaid for blocks and inner border
- ¾ yard of green plaid for blocks
- ¾ yard of green stripe for blocks
- ¾ yard of pink plaid B for blocks
- ¾ yard of yellow stripe for blocks
- ¾ yard of blue plaid for sashing
- 3 yards of fabric for backing
- ⅝ yard of pink for binding
- 54" x 73" piece of batting

Cutting

All measurements include ¼" seam allowances.

From each of the 4 plaids and 2 stripes for blocks, cut:
- 4 squares, 11" x 11", for a total of 24 squares

From the blue plaid, cut:
- 15 strips, 1½" x 42"; crosscut the strips into 58 strips, 1½" x 9"

From the scraps of the 4 plaids for blocks, cut:
- 15 squares, 1½" x 1½" (for the inner cornerstones)

From pink plaid A, cut:
- 1 strip, 1½" x 42"; crosscut into 20 squares, 1½" x 1½"
- 6 strips, 4" x 42"

From the yellow plaid, cut:
- 5 strips, 1½" x 42"
- 4 squares, 4" x 4"

From the pink binding fabric, cut:
- 7 strips, 2½" x 42"

Fabric Tips

Almost any group of small-scale prints will work in this quilt. I had a hard time choosing between a fun selection of contrasting polka-dot prints or plaids. The plaids won out in the end, but the polka dots are on the cutting board!

Making the Blocks

REFER TO "Making the Crazy Blocks" on pages 10–16 as needed.

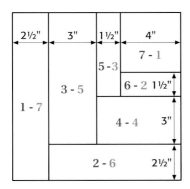

Block Cutting and Sewing Guide
Cut Size: 11" x 11"

1. Arrange the 24 squares into four decks of 6 each, alternating colors. Each deck should contain six different plaids. Secure the decks with a pin through all layers until ready to sew.

2. Referring to the block cutting and sewing guide, slice the decks. Work from one corner, moving the cut segments out of the line of cutting, but keeping them in order. Use a ruler to trim a 2½" strip off the top edge of the deck, move the cut segments away from the deck, and cut another 2½" strip off the next side.

3. Cut a 3" strip off the top edge of the deck, move the cut segments away from the deck, and cut another 3" strip off the next side.

4. Cut a 1½" strip off the top edge of the deck, move the cut segments away from the deck, and cut another 1½" strip off the next side.

5. Referring to the shuffling guide, shuffle the decks.

6. Make 24 blocks. Press the seam allowances toward the strip just added. Trim the blocks to 9" x 9".

Assembling the Quilt Top

1. Arrange the blocks in six horizontal rows of four blocks each with a 1½" x 9" sashing strip between each block. Move and turn the blocks until you're satisfied with the arrangement. Arrange the blocks so identical prints are not side by side in the finished layout.

Shuffling Guide

USE THE controlled shuffle described on page 14 for the decks in this quilt.

- Remove the top layer of center segment 1 and place on the bottom of the stack.
- Remove the top two layers of segments 2 and 3 and place them on the bottom of the stack.
- Remove the top three layers of segments 4 and 5 and place them on the bottom of the stack.
- Do not shuffle the outer segments 6 and 7.

2. Pin and sew the sashing strips and blocks together in rows. Press the seams toward the sashing strips.

Ace It!

You might want to number the block rows for reference when sewing them together for the quilt top.

3. Sew the 7 horizontal sashing rows using the remaining 1½" x 9" sashing strips and the 1½" x 1½" squares. Use pink plaid A squares for the top and bottom rows. For the inner rows, use pink plaid A squares on the outside and place squares from the scraps in the center as shown. Press seams toward the sashing.

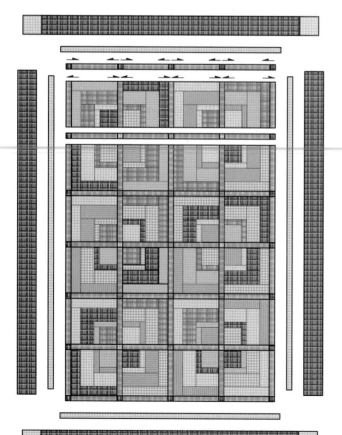

4. Sew the pieced sashing rows between the block rows. Press seams toward the sashing.

5. Sew the inner-border strips together to make one long strip. Refer to "Adding Borders" on page 18 to measure and cut the inner-border strips to size. Sew them to the sides of the quilt. Press the seams toward the border strips. Measure and sew the inner borders to the top and bottom.

6. Measure the width and length of the quilt, including the inner borders. Piece and cut the outer-border strips to those measurements. Sew the side borders to the quilt. Sew the 4" x 4" yellow plaid squares to each end of the remaining borders. Sew to the top and bottom of the quilt.

Finishing Your Quilt

REFER TO "Layering and Basting" on pages 19–21 and "Binding" on pages 21–22.

1. Divide the backing fabric crosswise into two panels, each approximately 54" long. Remove the selvages and sew the pieces together along the long edges to make the backing. Press the seam to one side.

2. Layer the quilt top with the batting and backing, with the backing seam parallel to the top and bottom edges of the quilt top. Baste the layers together.

3. Hand or machine quilt as desired.

4. Trim the backing and batting even with the quilt top and bind the quilt.

GARDEN PATH

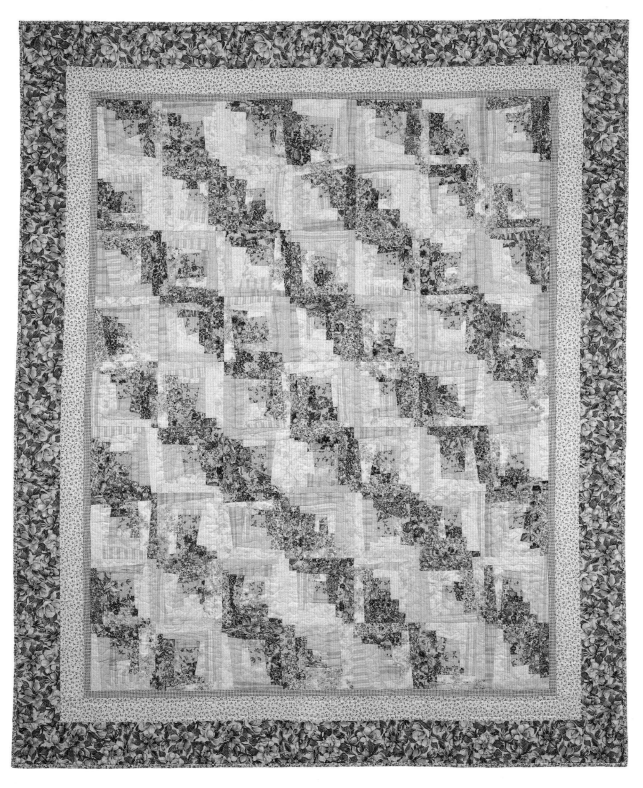

This block was designed as a twist on an old favorite, the Log Cabin. Instead of using just one tan fabric and one floral print, this quilt uses a bunch of each to produce a charming outcome.

FINISHED QUILT: 60½" x 73½" • FINISHED BLOCK: 6½" x 6½"

The abundance of flowers along a path in my back yard often inspires my creative spirit. The shapes of leaves and blossoms, along with the soft colors that flow together, prompted me to pull out the floral fabrics from my stash and design a quilt with meandering pathways among flowers.

Materials

Yardage is based on 42"-wide fabric

- 1⅛ yards of pink floral for outer border
- ¾ yard *each* of 6 different florals for blocks
- ¾ yard *each* of 6 different cream tone-on-tone prints for blocks
- ¾ yard of light green for block centers
- ⅝ yard of white and pink floral for middle border
- ⅜ yard of pink for inner border
- 3⅝ yards of fabric for backing
- ⅝ yard of fabric for binding
- 65" x 78" piece of batting

Fabric Tips

Think of small-scale floral prints in soft, warm colors. For the light (path) side of the blocks, choose a selection of tan prints and white prints in addition to tone-on-tone prints.

Cutting

All measurements include ¼" seam allowances.

From the 6 different florals, cut:
- 32 squares, 10½" x 10½"

From the 6 different cream prints, cut:
- 32 squares, 10½" x 10½"

From the light green fabric, cut:
- 6 strips, 3½" x 42"; crosscut the strips into 64 squares, 3½" x 3½"

From the pink fabric, cut:
- 6 strips, 1¼" x 42"

From the white and pink floral, cut:
- 6 strips, 2¾" x 42"

From the pink floral, cut:
- 7 strips, 5" x 42"

From the binding fabric, cut:
- 7 strips, 2½" x 42"

Making the Blocks

REFER TO "Making the Crazy Blocks" on pages 10–16 as needed.

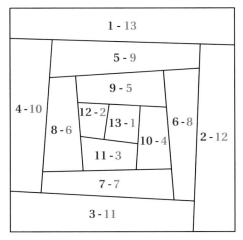

Block Cutting and Sewing Guide
Cut Size: 10½" x 10½"

1. Arrange the 64 squares of florals and cream prints into three decks of 12 each and two decks of 14 each, alternating the florals with the cream prints. Each deck should contain 12 different prints. For the two decks with 14 layers, you will have two duplicate fabric squares; make sure there are at least 6 layers separating them from one another. Secure the decks with a pin through all layers.

2. Referring to the block cutting and sewing guide, slice the decks. For easier cutting, separate each deck into two stacks. Cut the first stack using a paper template. Remove the template pieces and reassemble them on top of the second stack for cutting. Once cutting is complete, restack the two piles for shuffling.

3. Remove the centers of the stacks (segment 1). Use the center shapes as templates to cut new centers from the 3½" light green squares.

Shuffling Guide

USE THE controlled shuffle described on page 14 for the decks in this quilt to create a light side and a dark side.

- Segment 13: slide the top layer under the stack.
- Segment 12: slide the top 3 layers under the stack.
- Segment 11: slide the top 2 layers under the stack.
- Segment 10: slide the top 4 layers under the stack.
- Segment 9: slide the top 5 layers under the stack.
- Segment 8: slide the top 7 layers under the stack.

- Segment 7: slide the top 6 layers under the stack.
- Segment 6: slide the top 8 layers under the stack.
- Segment 5: slide the top 9 layers under the stack.
- Segment 4: slide the top 11 layers under the stack.
- Segment 3: slide the top 10 layers under the stack.
- Segment 2: do not shuffle.
- The centers are all the same, so they do not need to be shuffled.

Stack the light green squares and use the template to cut enough centers for each deck. Place the light green center pieces back in the stacks; be sure they are in the correct orientation and that the sides line up with the adjacent pieces.

4. Referring to the shuffling guide, shuffle the decks.

5. Make 64 blocks. Press seam allowances toward the outside strips, away from the center. Trim the blocks to 7" x 7". You will have one extra pieced block to use as an option when arranging the blocks.

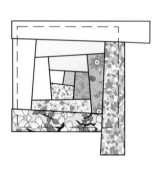

Assembling the Quilt Top

1. Arrange the blocks into nine horizontal rows of seven blocks each. Move and turn the blocks until you're satisfied with the arrangement. Try to arrange the blocks so identical prints are not side by side in the finished layout. You can arrange the blocks as I did in the diagonal furrows setting, or arrange them in any of the Log Cabin settings.

2. Sew the blocks into horizontal rows and press the seams in opposite directions from row to row. Sew the rows together and press the seams in one direction.

3. Sew the inner-border strips together to make one long strip. Refer to "Adding Borders" on page 18. Measure the quilt through the center and cut the inner-border strips to size. Sew them to the sides of the quilt. Press the seams toward the border strips. Measure, cut,

and add the inner borders to the top and bottom. Press. Repeat with the middle and outer borders.

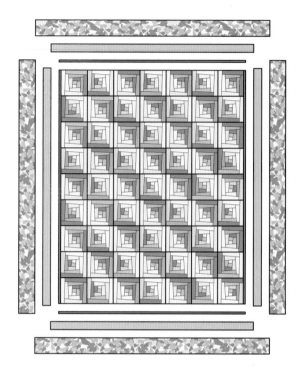

Finishing Your Quilt

REFER TO "Layering and Basting" on pages 19–21 and "Binding" on pages 21–22.

1. Divide the backing fabric crosswise into two panels, each approximately 65" long. Remove the selvages and sew the pieces together along the long edges to make the backing. Press the seam to one side.

2. Layer the quilt top with the batting and backing, with the backing seam parallel to the top and bottom of the quilt. Baste the layers together.

3. Hand or machine quilt as desired. I machine quilted mine using a straight, machine-guided stitch horizontally and vertically through the blocks. I also used a straight stitch for stitching the borders.

4. Trim the backing and batting even with the quilt top and bind the quilt.

SATURN

Self-bordered with its own blocks, this quilt throws a few simple squares into the mix of unmatched circles, which magically meet without matching, creating a cosmic Saturn.

FINISHED QUILT: 55½" x 70½" • FINISHED BLOCK: 7½" x 7½"

Another excuse to use batiks—that was the energy force behind this quilt. It's fast and easy, and you'll probably spend more time experimenting with the different layout possibilities than you will piecing it. It can be a beginner's dream if you choose to throw in more plain blocks than pieced. Or you can piece more blocks to create additional "planets with rings."

Materials

Yardage is based on 42"-wide fabric.

- ⅝ yard of green batik for inner border
- ⅜ yard *each* of 8 different peach and pink batiks for blocks
- ⅜ yard *each* of 8 different tan, brown, and green batiks for blocks
- 3⅜ yards fabric for backing
- ⅝ yard of fabric for binding
- 60" x 75" piece of batting

Fabric Tips

I chose a selection of contrasting batiks for this quilt. Hand-dyed fabrics paired with prints would create a different look. Or dip into your stash of Japanese fabrics for an Asian flair. It's especially important to use the 10-Foot Rule (page 9) and stand back to take a look at your selections to make sure they have that cosmic appearance.

Cutting

All measurements include ¼" seam allowances.

From each of the 16 batiks, cut:
- 1 strip, 9½" x 42"; crosscut each strip into 4 squares, 9½" x 9½", for a total of 64 squares

From the green batik, cut:
- 7 strips, 2" x 42"

From the binding fabric, cut:
- 7 strips, 2½" x 42"

Making the Blocks

REFER TO "Making the Crazy Blocks" on pages 10–16 as needed. In my quilt I used 14 of Block A and 42 of Block B. Feel free to vary the number of A and B blocks as you prefer.

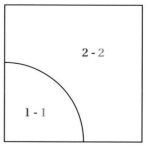

Block A
Cutting and Sewing Guide
Cut Size: 9½" x 9½"

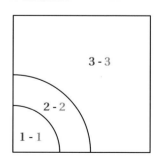

Block B
Cutting and Sewing Guide
Cut Size: 9½" x 9½"

1. Arrange 56 squares into seven decks of 8 each, alternating the pink and peach with the tan, brown, and green. Each deck should contain eight different prints. You will have 8 remaining squares to use as solid blocks for

the quilt layout. Secure the decks with a pin through all layers until ready to sew.

2. Referring to the block cutting and sewing guide, slice the decks. Slice two decks for Block A and five decks for Block B. This will give you 16 A blocks and 40 B blocks.

Ace It!

Always use a ruler when cutting curves with a rotary cutter. I just slide it along the curve, cutting only about 1" as I go. The more you get accustomed to this, the faster it goes.

---

3. Shuffle the decks, referring to "Traditional Shuffling" on page 13. (For the Block A decks, follow steps 1 and 2 on page 13.)

4. Make 56 blocks. Note that the sewing order for these blocks is the same as the cutting order. You will have one extra pieced block to use as an option when arranging the blocks. Press seam allowances toward the center arc. Trim the blocks to 8" x 8". Trim the solid squares to 8" x 8".

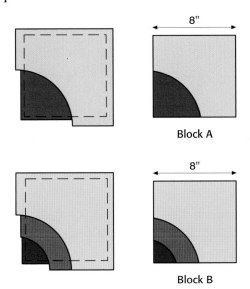

Block A

Block B

Assembling the Quilt Top

1. Arrange the pieced blocks and squares into nine horizontal rows of seven blocks each. Move and turn the blocks until you're satisfied with the arrangement. You will have extra squares to use as options. Try to arrange the blocks so identical prints are not side by side in the finished layout. Look through a door peephole or use the 10-foot rule to check the color and block balance.

2. Sew the inner-border strips together into one long strip. Cut the long strip into two strips, 2" x 53"; two strips, 2" x 56"; and four strips, 2" x 8".

3. Lay the sashing strips along the inside edge of the outer row of blocks. The outer row of blocks will become the border. Use the 2" x 53" strips for each side and the 2" x 56" strips for the top and bottom. Place the four shorter strips vertically, inside the edge of the four corner blocks.

4. For the inside portion of the quilt, sew the blocks into seven horizontal rows with five blocks in each. Press the seams in opposite directions from row to row. Sew the rows together and press the seams in one direction.

5. Sew the blocks for the border together; press seams in one direction. Add the 2" x 53" inner-border strips to each side of the quilt top. Press seams toward the inner border. Add the block borders to each side of the quilt top. Press all seams toward the inner border as shown. Sew the 2" x 56" inner-border strips to both the top and bottom edges of the quilt top; press.

6. Sew a 2" x 8" strip to each end of the top and bottom row and press. Add the corner blocks onto each end of the borders. Add the top and bottom borders to the quilt. Press.

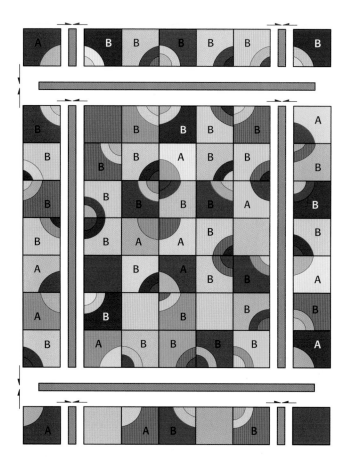

Finishing Your Quilt

REFER TO "Layering and Basting" on pages 19–21 and "Binding" on pages 21–22.

1. Divide the backing fabric crosswise into two panels, each approximately 60" long. Remove the selvages and sew the pieces together along two long edges to make the backing. Press the seam to one side.

2. Layer the quilt top with the batting and backing, with the backing seam parallel to the top and bottom of the quilt. Baste the layers together.

3. Hand or machine quilt as desired. I machine quilted mine using an overall stipple in the blocks and stitched the borders in the ditch.

4. Trim the backing and batting even with the quilt top and bind the quilt.

SALSA

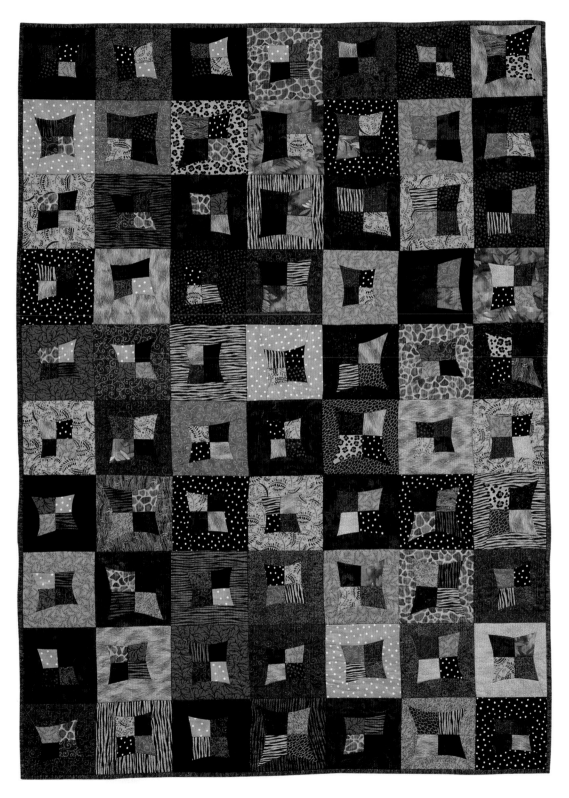

This quilt is a favorite of mine, bursting with loads of flavorful color.
The challenge here is to pick as many contrasting fabrics as you can.

FINISHED QUILT: 45½" x 65" • FINISHED BLOCK: 6½" x 6½"

The framed, uneven little Four Patch blocks in this quilt are a snap to make. I decided to jazz things up by using some jungle prints I had stashed away. The result is a spicy quilt that I named "Salsa."

Materials

Yardage is based on 42"-wide fabric.

- ⅜ yard *each* of 9 different warm colors (golds, reds, and tans) for blocks
- ⅜ yard *each* of 9 different cool colors (blues, greens, purples, and black) for blocks
- 2⅞ yards of fabric for backing
- ⅝ yard of fabric for binding
- 50" x 70" piece of batting

Cutting

All measurements include ¼" seam allowances.

From each of the 18 different fabrics, cut:

- 1 strip, 9" x 42"; crosscut into a total of 70 squares, 9" x 9"

From the binding fabric, cut:

- 6 strips, 2½" x 42"

Fabric Tips

I chose a selection of jungle prints from my stash and then added splashes of contrasting greens, reds, and purples, along with some inky black prints. Strong colors work well, but avoid large-scale prints.

Making the Blocks

REFER TO "Making the Crazy Blocks" on pages 10–16 as needed.

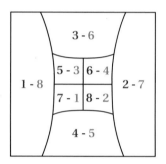

Block Cutting and Sewing Guide
Cut Size: 9" x 9"

1. Arrange the 70 squares into seven decks of 10 each, alternating colors. Each deck should contain 10 different prints. Secure the decks with a pin through all layers until ready to sew.

2. Referring to the block cutting and sewing guide, slice the decks. Cut an arc shape off the side edges first. Move the cut segments out of the way and cut an arc shape off the remaining two sides.

3. Move the cut segments out of the way and cut the remaining segments once through the center vertically and once through the center horizontally, creating an irregular four-patch unit.

4. Referring to the shuffling guide, shuffle the decks.

Shuffling Guide

Use the controlled shuffle described on page 14 for the decks in this quilt.

- Shuffle only the four center segments in the traditional manner; refer to "Traditional Shuffling" on page 13.
- Do not shuffle the arcs on the outside edges.

5. Make 70 blocks. Chain-piece segments 1 and 2 together and segments 3 and 4 together. Clip apart and press the seams of segments 1 and 2 in the opposite direction of segments 3 and 4. Sew segments 1–2 and segments 3–4 together to make a four-patch unit. Replace the segments on the paper layout and complete the sewing, following the block cutting and sewing guide. Press seam allowances toward the outside strips, away from the center. Trim the blocks to 7" x 7".

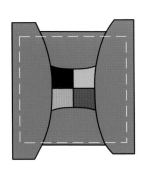 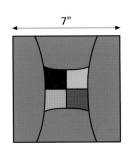

7"

Assembling the Quilt Top

1. Arrange the blocks into 10 horizontal rows of seven blocks each. Move and turn the blocks until you're satisfied with the arrangement. Try to arrange the blocks so identical prints are not side by side in the finished layout. Look through a door peephole or use the 10-foot rule to check the color and block balance.

2. Sew the blocks into horizontal rows and press the seams in opposite directions from row to row. Sew the rows together and press the seams in one direction.

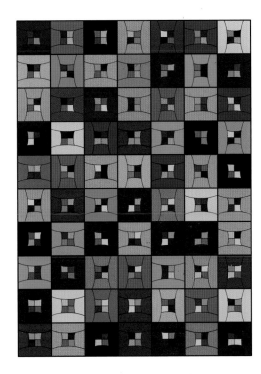

Finishing Your Quilt

Refer to "Layering and Basting" on pages 19–21 and "Binding" on pages 21–22.

1. Divide the backing fabric in half crosswise to create two panels, each approximately 51" long. Remove the selvages and sew the pieces together along the long edges to make the backing. Press the seam to one side.

2. Layer the quilt top with the batting and backing, with the backing seam parallel to the top and bottom of the quilt. Baste the layers together.

3. Hand or machine quilt as desired.

4. Trim the backing and batting even with the quilt top and bind the quilt.

RED ONION

In this quilt, swirling layers upon layers peel away. It's easy and mesmerizing, all at the same time.
The fast-pieced border technique could be used for almost any quilt.

FINISHED QUILT: 52" x 69" • FINISHED BLOCK: 8½" x 8½"

The swirls of color in this quilt remind me of gently rolling farm fields, viewed from above through the window of an airplane. The quilt is really quite easy to make; the blocks are trimmed to size after the curves have been sewn. The result is a sophisticated yet simple design.

Materials

Yardage is based on 42"-wide fabric.

- ½ yard *each* of 6 different batiks in light green and tan for blocks
- ½ yard *each* of 6 different batiks in dark purple, brown, and green for blocks
- ½ yard of purple batik for inner border
- ¼ yard *each* of 5 different batiks in light green and tan for outer border
- ¼ yard *each* of 5 different batiks in dark purple, brown, and green for outer border
- 3¼ yards of fabric for backing
- ⅝ yard of fabric for binding
- 57" x 74" piece of batting

Fabric Tips

Choose a rich selection of tan, green, and purple batiks, with purple being the darkest value. Or select a combination of your three favorite colors, one light, one medium, and one dark.

Cutting

All measurements include ¼" seam allowances.

From each of the 12 batiks for the blocks, cut:
- 1 strip, 12" x 42"; crosscut into 3 squares, 12" x 12", for a total of 36 squares

From the purple batik, cut:
- 6 strips, 2" x 42"

From each of the 10 batiks for borders, cut:
- 1 strip, 4" x 42"; crosscut into a total of 30 rectangles, 4" x 13"

From the binding fabric, cut:
- 7 strips, 2½" x 42"

Making the Blocks

REFER TO "Making the Crazy Blocks" on pages 10–16 as needed.

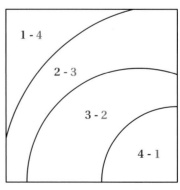

Block Cutting and Sewing Guide
Cut Size: 12" x 12"

1. Arrange the 36 squares into six decks of 6 each, alternating lights and darks. Each deck should contain six different prints. Secure the decks with a pin through all layers until ready to sew.

2. Referring to the block cutting and sewing guide, slice the decks.

3. Shuffle the decks, using the traditional shuffle described on page 13.

4. Make 36 blocks. Press the seam allowances toward the small arc. Trim the blocks to 9" x 9". You will have 1 extra block to use as an option.

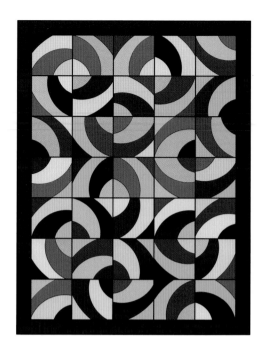

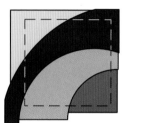

Assembling the Quilt Top

1. Arrange the blocks into seven horizontal rows of five blocks each. Move and turn the blocks until you're satisfied with the arrangement. Try to arrange the blocks so identical prints are not side by side in the finished layout.

2. Sew the blocks into horizontal rows and press the seams in opposite directions from row to row. Sew the rows together and press the seams in one direction.

3. Sew the inner-border strips together to make one long strip. Refer to "Adding Borders" on page 18. Measure the quilt through the center and cut the inner-border strips to size. Sew them to the sides of the quilt. Press the seams toward the border strips. Measure and cut the top and bottom inner-border strips and sew them to the quilt.

4. To make the outer border, arrange the 4" x 13" rectangles into five decks of six each, alternating colors and values. Make six random vertical cuts, varying the angle and width slightly from deck to deck. Shuffle using a traditional shuffle, and sew together in units of six. Trim the top and bottom edges even.

Border Cutting and Sewing Guide
Cut Size: 4" x 13"

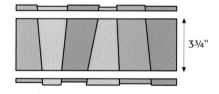

3¾"

5. Piece the border units together to make one long strip. Measure, cut, and sew the borders as you did for the inner borders. If you want to miter the border corners as in the quilt shown, see "Mitered Border Option" at right.

Mitered Border Option

1. Follow steps 4 and 5 and piece the outer-border units together to make one long strip.

2. Measure the quilt through the center and add 4". Cut the border strips to those measurements.

3. Fold the borders in half to find the exact center; lightly press a crease as a guideline. Start from the center guideline and measure out a distance equal to one-half the finished quilt length, back up ¼" (for seam allowance), and mark with a pin. Repeat in the opposite direction.

4. On the wrong side of the quilt, mark the center of all four sides and ¼" in from the edge of each corner. With right sides together, match and pin the marked points of the border to the quilt top.

5. Sew the border to the quilt from match point to match point, backstitching at each end. Repeat for the remaining borders.

6. Fold the quilt top, diagonally with right sides together so the borders are aligned at the corners, and pin together. Use a ruler and place the edge against the fold. Draw a diagonal line, along the edge of the ruler, on the border from the match point to the edge of the border strip.

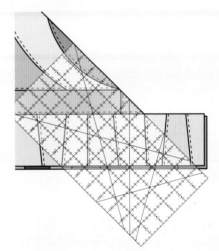

7. Begin with a backstitch at the inside corner and stitch on the marked line to the outside edge. Check the right side of the quilt to make sure the seams are aligned. Trim excess fabric from the borders, leaving a ¼" seam allowance. Press the seam open.

Finishing Your Quilt

REFER TO "Layering and Basting" on pages 19–21 and "Binding" on pages 21–22.

1. Divide the backing fabric crosswise into two panels, each approximately 58" long. Remove the selvages and sew the pieces together along two long edges to make the backing. Press the seam to one side.

2. Layer the quilt top with the batting and backing, with the backing seam parallel to the top and bottom of the quilt. Baste the layers together.

3. Hand or machine quilt as desired.

4. Trim the backing and batting even with the quilt top and bind the quilt.

AUNT BESSIE'S KALEIDOSCOPE

I made this quilt with my sweet Aunt Bessie in mind. She always greeted me with open arms and always wore a dress covered by an apron made of fabrics similar to those in this quilt.

FINISHED QUILT: 42" x 56½" • FINISHED BLOCK: 6" x 6"

This quilt was inspired by my Great Aunt Bessie. Over the top of her dresses, she always wore an old-fashioned, full-length apron stitched from what looked like feed sacks. Memories of her sweet hugs and my fascination with her collection of trinkets from years gone by will always warm my heart.

Materials

Yardage is based on 42"-wide fabric.

- ⅝ yard of muslin for outer sashing
- ½ yard of green plaid for inner sashing and corner squares
- ⅜ yard *each* of 2 different green prints for blocks
- ⅜ yard *each* of 2 different yellows for blocks
- ⅜ yard *each* of 2 different pinks for blocks
- ⅜ yard *each* of 2 different purples for blocks
- ⅜ yard *each* of 2 different blues for blocks
- ⅜ yard *each* of 2 different reds for blocks
- 2⅝ yards of fabric for backing
- ⅝ yard of red for binding
- 46" x 61" piece of batting

Note: I used more than two different prints of each color in my quilt. Purchase more than two different fabrics if you want a scrappier quilt.

Fabric Tips

A balance of small-scale '30s prints in all colors is the key to this old-fashioned quilt. But you could use any sort of fabric. Just be sure there is enough contrast between your chosen fabrics so that the arcs will show up against the backgrounds.

Cutting

All measurements include ¼" seam allowances.

From each of the 12 fabrics, cut:
- 1 strip, 8½" x 42"; crosscut into 4 squares, 8½" x 8½", for a total of 48 squares

From the green plaid, cut:
- 8 strips, 1½" x 42"; crosscut into 48 rectangles, 1½" x 6½"
- 6 squares, 2" x 2"

From the muslin, cut:
- 9 strips, 2" x 42"; crosscut into 17 strips, 2" x 13½"

From the yellow scraps, cut:
- 12 squares, 1½" x 1½"

From the red fabric, cut:
- 6 strips, 2½" x 42"

Making the Blocks

REFER TO "Making the Crazy Blocks" on pages 10–16 as needed.

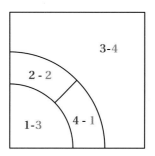

Block Cutting and Sewing Guide
Cut Size: 8½" x 8½"

1. Arrange the 48 squares into eight decks of 6 each, alternating colors. Each deck should contain six different prints. Secure the decks with a pin through all layers until ready to sew.

2. Referring to the block cutting and sewing guide, slice the decks.

3. Referring to the shuffling guide, shuffle the decks.

4. Make 48 blocks. Press seam allowances toward the outside strips, away from the center. Trim the blocks to 6½" x 6½".

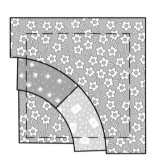 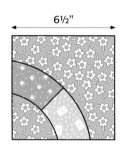

Shuffling Guide

USE THE controlled shuffle described on page 14 for the decks in this quilt.

- Remove the top layer of segment 1 and place it on the bottom of the stack.
- Remove the top two layers of segment 2 and place them on the bottom of the stack.
- Do not shuffle segments 3 and 4.

Assembling the Quilt Top

1. Arrange the blocks in 12 sets of four each. Turn the blocks so that the small arcs are inward, creating a circle. Once you're satisfied with the arrangement, add the 1½" x 6½" green plaid sashing strips between the blocks and a 1½" x 1½" yellow square in the center.

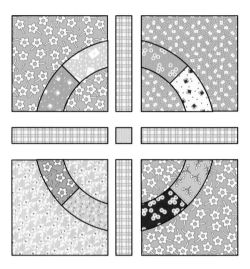

2. Pin and sew each set of blocks and sashing strips together into two horizontal rows. Press the seams toward the sashing. Sew the remaining two sashing strips together with the yellow square in the middle. Press seams toward the sashing. Pin and sew the two horizontal rows together with the pieced sashing strip between. Press the seams toward the sashing strips.

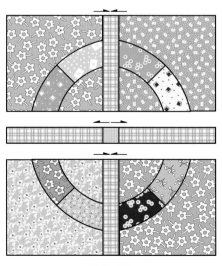

Make 12.

3. Arrange the block units into four horizontal rows of three each. Sew the horizontal rows together with a 2" x 13½" muslin sashing strip between each set. Number the block rows for reference when sewing them together for the quilt top.

4. Sew three 2" x 13½" muslin sashing strips together with a 2" x 2" green plaid cornerstone between each. Repeat to make three rows.

5. Sew the block rows together with the pieced sashing rows. Press seams toward the sashing.

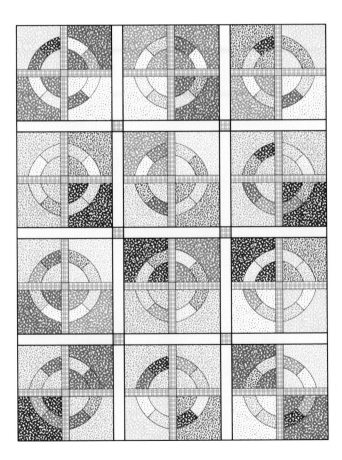

Finishing Your Quilt

REFER TO "Layering and Basting" on pages 19–21 and "Binding" on pages 21–22.

1. Divide the backing fabric crosswise into two panels, each approximately 47" long. Remove the selvages and sew the pieces together along two long edges to make the backing. Press the seam to one side.

2. Layer the quilt top with the batting and backing, with the backing seam parallel to the top and bottom of the quilt. Baste the layers together.

3. Hand or machine quilt as desired.

4. Trim the backing and batting even with the quilt top and bind the quilt.

HOPSCOTCH

*This quilt for kids is fun to make. Each block starts out as four smaller blocks
that are sewn together, and then sliced and spliced back together again.*

FINISHED QUILT: 52" x 70" • FINISHED BLOCK: 16" x 16"

$\mathcal{I}$ decided to design a quilt with kids in mind—one that was so bright it would always be easy to find. An added benefit is that if it gets colored on, you'll never notice! Keep it handy to take along in the car on day trips and special visits.

Materials

Yardage is based on 42"-wide fabric.

- 1⅛ yards of black print for inner sashing
- ¾ yard of blue print for sashing
- ⅜ yard *each* of 2 different purples for blocks
- ⅜ yard *each* of 2 different yellows for blocks
- ⅜ yard *each* of 2 different blues for blocks
- ⅜ yard *each* of 2 different oranges for blocks
- ⅜ yard *each* of 2 different turquoises for blocks
- ⅜ yard *each* of 2 different reds for blocks
- 3⅛ yards of fabric for backing
- ⅝ yard of purple for binding
- 56" x 74" piece of batting

Fabric Tips

Choose fun prints with kids in mind—stripes, dots, swirls—most anything bright and outrageous goes. Once you have a good selection of contrasting colors, choose a black print for the sashing and then stand back and take a look, using the 10-Foot Rule (page 9).

Cutting

All measurements include ¼" seam allowances.

From each of the 12 fabrics, cut:
- 1 strip, 9" x 42"; crosscut each strip into 4 squares, 9" x 9", for a total of 48 squares

From the black print, cut:
- 24 strips, 1½" x 42"; crosscut into 24 strips, 1½" x 14½", and 24 strips, 1½" x 16½"

From the blue print, cut:
- 8 strips, 2½" x 42"; crosscut 4 of the strips into 8 strips, 2½" x 16½"

From the purple fabric, cut:
- 7 strips, 2½" x 42"

Making the Blocks

REFER TO "Making the Crazy Blocks" on pages 10–16 as needed.

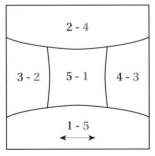

Block Cutting and Sewing Guide
Cut Size: 9" x 9"

1. Arrange the 48 squares into 12 decks of 4 each; each deck should contain only two different fabrics, alternated with each other. Secure the decks with a pin through all layers until ready to sew.

2. Referring to the block cutting and sewing guide, slice the decks.

3. Referring to the shuffling guide, shuffle the decks.

4. Make 48 blocks. Follow the numerical sewing order on the sewing guide. Press seam allowances toward the outside strips, away from the center. Trim the blocks to 7½" x 7½".

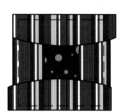 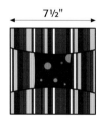

Shuffling Guide

USE THE controlled shuffle described on page 14 for the decks in this quilt.

- Remove the top layer of center segment 1 and place it on the bottom of the deck.
- Do not shuffle any other segments.

Assembling the Quilt Top

1. Arrange and sew the blocks into 12 sets of four each. Each set should have only two color combinations.

2. Measure and cut the blocks apart 3¾" above and below the horizontal center seam, separating the pieced block into three sections.

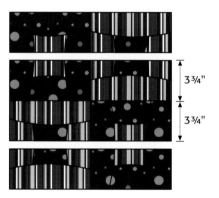

3. Pin and sew two of the 1½" x 14½" black strips between each of the cut blocks, sewing the block set back together. Press seams toward the black strips.

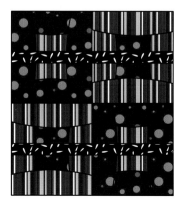

4. Cut the block set apart again in the opposite direction, 3¾" on each side of the center seam. Pin and sew two 1½" x 16½" black strips between each of the cut block sections, sewing the block set back together. Press seams toward the black strips.

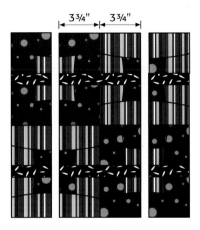

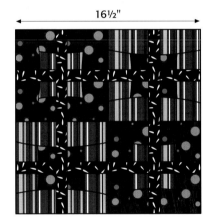

5. Arrange the block units into four horizontal rows of three units each. Sew the horizontal rows together with a 2½" blue print sashing strip between each set. Press the seams toward the sashing.

6. Remove the selvages and piece the remaining four blue print sashing strips together into one long piece. Cut the long strip into three strips, 2½" x 52½".

7. Pin and sew the blue print sashing strips between the four horizontal rows. Press seams toward the sashing.

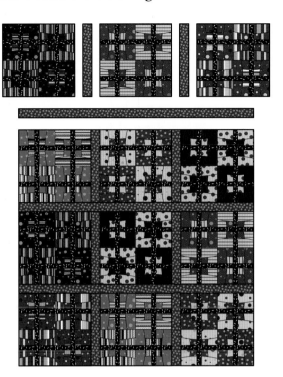

Finishing Your Quilt

REFER TO "Layering and Basting" on pages 19–21 and "Binding" on pages 21–22.

1. Divide the backing fabric crosswise into two panels, each approximately 56" long. Remove the selvages and sew the pieces together along two long edges to make the backing. Press the seam to one side.

2. Layer the quilt top with the batting and backing, with the backing seam parallel to the top and bottom of the quilt. Baste the layers together.

3. Hand or machine quilt as desired.

4. Trim the backing and batting even with the quilt top and bind the quilt.

SUSHI

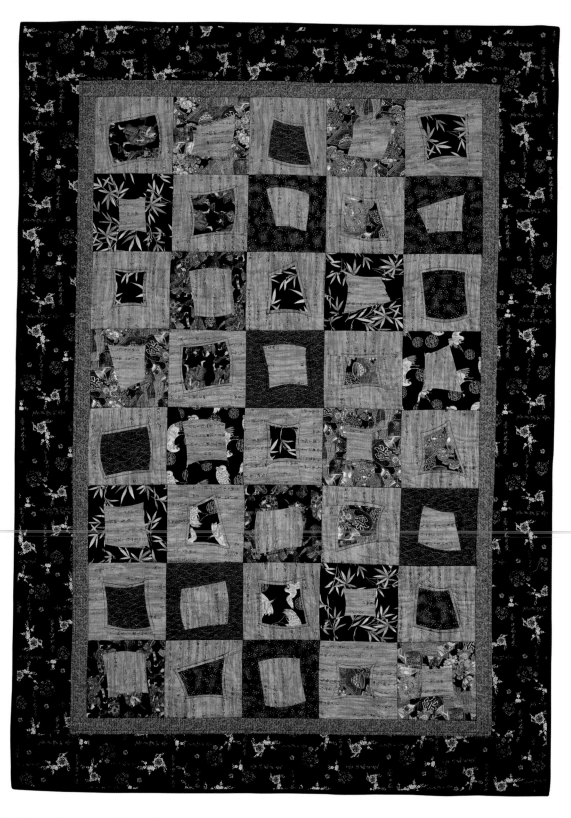

The fabric selection is what makes this a truly wonderful quilt. In addition to the fun fabric, it's a breeze to make!
FINISHED QUILT: 51½" x 74" • FINISHED BLOCK: 7½" x 7½"

I couldn't leave my local quilt shop without making a purchase of some of the awesome and irresistible Asian prints. I designed this quilt to "fit" the fabric; it was so easy, fun, and fast that I immediately made another one!

Materials

Yardage is based on 42"-wide fabric.

- 2⅛ yards of blue-green for blocks
- 1¼ yards of black print for outer border
- ½ yard of coral for inner border
- ⅜ yard *each* of 5 different black prints for blocks
- ⅜ yard of coral and black print for blocks
- ⅜ yard of purple and turquoise print for blocks
- 3⅛ yards of fabric for backing
- ⅝ yard of black for binding
- 56" x 78" piece of batting

Fabric Tips

I used an incredible sea-foam blue Asian print as a guide to choosing the remaining prints. The dark fabrics are a combination of black backgrounds accented with gold. The large-scale Asian prints have turquoise, crimson, and gold accents. Both the dark and large-scale prints need to contrast with your starting fabric. This design works well with both subtle prints and large-scale prints.

Cutting

All measurements include ¼" seam allowances.

From the blue-green fabric, cut:
- 5 strips, 10" x 42"; crosscut the strips into 20 squares, 10" x 10"

From each of the remaining prints for blocks, cut:
- 1 strip, 10" x 42"; crosscut the strips into 20 squares, 10" x 10"

From the coral fabric, cut:
- 6 strips, 2" x 42"

From the black print for outer border, cut:
- 6 strips, 6" x 42"

From the binding fabric, cut:
- 7 strips, 2½" x 42"

Making the Blocks

REFER TO "Making the Crazy Blocks" on pages 10–16 as needed.

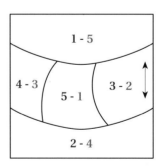

Block Cutting and Sewing Guide
Cut Size: 9" x 9"

1. Arrange the 40 squares into 10 decks of 4 each; each deck should contain three different fabrics. Alternate 2 of the green squares with two other prints. Secure the decks with a pin through all layers until ready to sew.

Shuffling Guide

Use the controlled shuffle described on page 14 for the decks in this quilt.

- Remove the top layer of segment 1 and place it on the bottom of the stack.
- Don't shuffle any other segments.

2. Referring to the block cutting and sewing guide, slice the decks.

3. Referring to the shuffling guide, shuffle the decks.

4. Make 40 blocks, following the numerical sewing order on the block cutting and sewing guide. Press seam allowances toward the outside strips, away from the center. Trim the blocks to 8" x 8".

 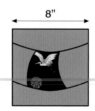

Assembling the Quilt Top

1. Arrange the blocks into eight horizontal rows of five blocks each. Move and turn the blocks until you're satisfied with the arrangement. Look through a door peephole or use the 10-foot rule to check the color and block balance.

2. Sew the blocks into horizontal rows and press the seams in opposite directions from row to row. Sew the rows together and press the seams in one direction.

3. Sew the coral inner-border strips together to make one long strip. Refer to "Adding Borders" on page 18. Measure the quilt through the center and cut the inner-border strips to size. Sew them to the sides of the quilt. Press the seams toward the border strips. Measure and cut the top and bottom inner-border strips and sew them to the quilt. Repeat for the outer border.

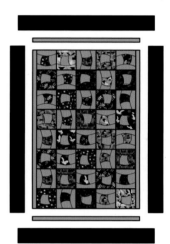

Finishing Your Quilt

Refer to "Layering and Basting" on pages 19–21 and "Binding" on pages 21–22.

1. Divide the backing fabric crosswise into two panels, each approximately 56" long. Remove the selvages and sew the pieces together along the long edges to make the backing. Press the seam to one side.

2. Layer the quilt top with the batting and backing, with the backing seam parallel to the top and bottom of the quilt. Baste the layers together using your favorite method.

3. Hand or machine quilt as desired. I machine quilted mine in straight lines in the ditch around the blocks and outlined the block centers. I also stitched straight parallel lines in the borders.

4. Trim the backing and batting even with the quilt top and bind the quilt.

JOKER'S WILD

The blocks in this quilt only look tricky—they're very easy to make. Look for lots of fun, contrasting colors and try your hand!

FINISHED QUILT: 62" x 82" • FINISHED BLOCK: 4½" x 6½"

An entertaining joker found in a deck of cards was the inspiration for this unusual and rather wild quilt. It's made up of three different but very easy blocks. The uneven hearts and diamonds are a blast to make. It's so much fun to see how each block will turn out.

Materials

Yardage is based on 42"-wide fabric.

- 1⅛ yards of purple print for outer border
- 1 yard of black print for sashing
- ¾ yard of turquoise for inner border
- ⅜ yard *each* of 4 different lime greens for triangle blocks
- ⅜ yard *each* of 2 different golds for diamond and heart blocks
- ⅜ yard *each* of 2 different blues for diamond and heart blocks
- ⅜ yard *each* of 2 different reds for triangle blocks
- ⅜ yard *each* of 2 different turquoise prints for diamond and heart blocks
- ⅜ yard *each* of 2 different purples for triangle blocks
- ⅜ yard *each* of 2 different reds for diamond and heart blocks
- ⅜ yard *each* of 2 different purples for diamond and heart blocks
- 5 yards of fabric for backing
- ¾ yard of fabric for binding
- 66" x 86" piece of batting

MATERIALS FOR JOKER APPLIQUÉ

- One 5" x 5" square each of the following colors:

    Gold for outer hat
    Purple for inner hat
    Dark purple for collar
    Moss green for face
    Dark pink for outer crown
    Dark red for inner crown
    Dark red for diamond on face
    Blue for background diamonds

Cutting

All measurements include ¼" seam allowances.

From each of the 8 fabrics for triangle blocks, cut:

- 1 strip, 7½" x 42"; crosscut into 6 rectangles, 5½" x 7½". Cut 1 extra rectangle from 1 strip for a total of 49.

From each of the 10 different fabrics for diamond and heart blocks, cut:

- 1 strip, 9" x 42"; crosscut into 5 rectangles, 7" x 9", for a total of 50

From the turquoise fabric for inner border, cut;

- 1 rectangle, 7" x 9"
- 7 strips, 2" x 42"

From the black print, cut:

- 18 strips, 1½" x 42"; crosscut 7 into 20 strips, 1½" x 13½"; crosscut 5 into 20 strips, 1½" x 9½"

From the block scraps, cut:

- 20 squares, 1½" x 1½"

From the purple print, cut:

- 8 strips, 4½" x 42"

From the binding fabric, cut:

- 8 strips, 2½" x 42"

Fabric Tips

Set the scene for the joker by choosing rich contrasting colors of red, turquoise, purple, and gold set off with brilliant splashes of green. Add an inky black to the mixture for the sashing and then stand back and take a look, using the 10-Foot Rule (page 9). Stick with mainly tone-on-tone prints for this quilt.

Making the Pieced Blocks

REFER TO "Making the Crazy Blocks" on pages 10–16 as needed.

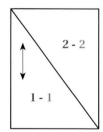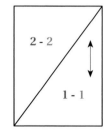

Triangle Block Cutting and Sewing **Guide**
Cut Size: 5½" x 7½"
Cut 3 decks in each direction.

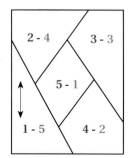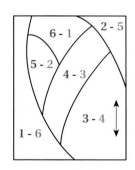

Small Diamond Block Cutting and Sewing **Guide**
Cut Size: 7" x 9"

Heart Block Cutting and Sewing **Guide**
Cut Size: 7" x 9"

1. For the triangle blocks that will make up the large diamonds, arrange 24 lime green 5½" x 7½" rectangles with the 24 rectangles of assorted other colors into eight decks of 6 each. Each deck should contain three different greens alternated with three other colors. Secure the decks with a pin through all layers until ready to sew. You will have one extra rectangle to use for the joker appliqué block.

2. Referring to the block cutting and sewing guide, slice the decks. Cut the 5½" x 7½" rectangles in half diagonally from corner to corner; cut four decks in reverse.

3. Referring to the shuffling guide, shuffle the decks.

4. Make 48 blocks from the triangles. Press seams toward the dark fabric. Trim to 5" x 7".

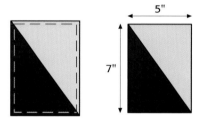

5. For the small diamond blocks, arrange an assortment of 25 rectangles, 7" x 9", into five decks of 5 each. Each deck should have an assortment of contrasting colors. Secure the decks with a pin through all layers until ready to sew.

Ace It!

You may want to gently finger-press the blocks before trimming. When you join the four triangle units to create the large diamonds, you may need to press the seams again in opposite directions so that they will butt together.

6. Slice the decks. I varied the cutting from deck to deck so that some diamonds are larger than others. Shuffle, referring to the shuffling guide. Make 25 diamond blocks. Press seams away from the center diamond. Trim the blocks to 5" x 7".

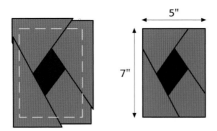

7. For the heart blocks, arrange an assortment of 13 brights alternated with 13 darks into three decks of 6 and one deck of 8. Secure the decks with a pin through all layers until ready to sew.

8. Slice the decks, following the block cutting and sewing guide. Shuffle, referring to the shuffling guide. Make 26 heart blocks. Press seams for hearts to one side. Trim the blocks to 5" x 7".

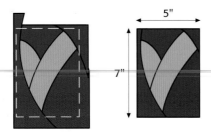

Shuffling Guide

Use the controlled shuffle described on page 14 for the triangle decks.

- Shuffle the segments on one side of each deck once.
- Do not shuffle the segments on the opposite side.

Use a controlled shuffle for the small diamond decks.
- Shuffle the center segments once.
- Do not shuffle the remaining segments.

Use a controlled shuffle for the heart decks.
- Shuffle segments 2 and 3 one time each.
- Do not shuffle the remaining segments.

Making the Appliqué Block

1. Refer to "Fusible-Web Appliqué" on pages 18–19. Use the appliqué pattern on page 70 and prepare the appliqué shapes.

2. Referring to the pattern illustration, position, fuse, and stitch the appliqué in place on the remaining 5½" x 7½" background rectangle. I used a straight stitch around the edges of the appliqué.

3. Trim the block to 5" x 7".

Assembling the Quilt Top

1. Separate the triangle blocks into 12 sets of four each. Arrange each set into two horizontal rows of two each to make the large diamond blocks. Keep the green on the outside corners of the blocks. Sew the two rows together, and press seams in opposite directions. Pin and sew the rows together, and press seams in one direction. Make 12 blocks.

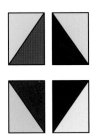 

Make 12.

2. Arrange two heart blocks together with two small diamond blocks for a total of 13 sets. One set should include the Joker block in place of a small diamond block. Arrange each set into two horizontal rows of two each, with a heart in the upper left and lower right; the diamonds should be in the upper right and lower left.

3. Sew the two rows together, and press seams in opposite directions. Pin and sew the rows together; press seams in one direction. Make 13 sets.

4. Arrange the block sets as shown in the photo and in the quilt diagram, with five horizontal rows of five blocks each. The heart and small diamond block sets should be in the corners and should alternate with the large pieced diamonds.

5. Sew the horizontal rows together with a black 1½" x 13½" sashing strip between each block set. Press seams toward the sashing.

6. Piece five sashing strips, 1½" x 9½", together with an assortment of four corner squares, 1½" x 1½". Make four sashing rows; press seams toward the sashing.

7. Pin and sew a pieced sashing row between each of the horizontal rows. Press seams toward the sashing.

8. Piece the remaining sashing strips together to make one long strip. Measure the quilt through the middle and cut strips for the sides, top, and bottom.

9. Sew the sashing strips to the sides of the quilt. Press toward the sashing.

10. Sew a 1½" x 1½" square to each end of the remaining two black sashing strips; press toward the sashing. Pin and sew to the top and bottom of the quilt. Press seams toward the sashing.

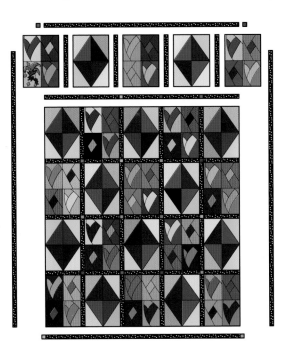

11. Sew the turquoise inner-border strips together to make one long strip. Cut the inner-border strips to size and sew them to the quilt top as directed in "Adding Borders" on page 18. Press the seams toward the border strips. Repeat for the outer border.

Finishing Your Quilt

Refer to "Layering and Basting" on pages 19–21 and "Binding" on pages 21–22.

1. Divide the backing fabric crosswise into two panels, each approximately 90" long. Remove the selvages and sew the pieces together along two long edges to make the backing. Press the seam to one side.

2. Layer the quilt top with the batting and backing, with the backing seam parallel to the sides of the quilt. Baste the layers together.

3. Hand or machine quilt as desired.

4. Trim the backing and batting even with the quilt top and bind the quilt.

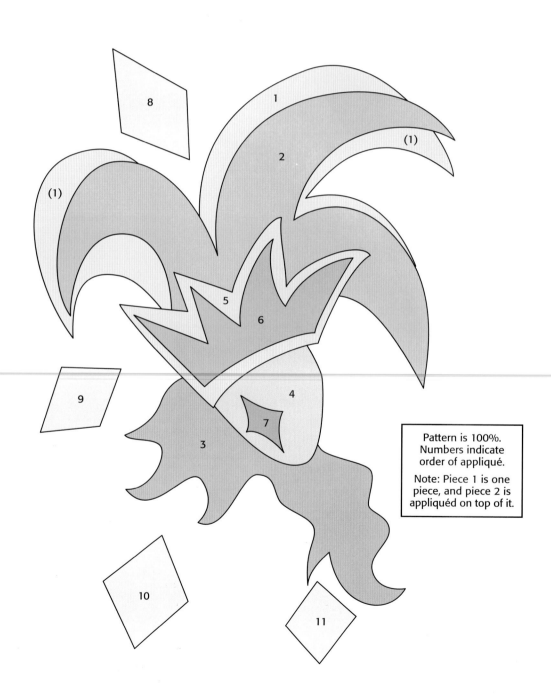

Pattern is 100%.
Numbers indicate order of appliqué.

Note: Piece 1 is one piece, and piece 2 is appliquéd on top of it.

OLD GLORY

With all the wonderful patriotic fabrics available, it's almost impossible not to buy! The selections got the best of me, again, and I just had to put them all together for that "united" look.

FINISHED QUILT: 73" x 88" • FINISHED BLOCK: 7½" x 7½"

The glorious red, white, and blue prints just keep coming! Once again, they ended up in my stash, and of course I had to design a quilt just for them. The images in the light conversation prints add patriotic images, while the red and blue prints line up to form the diamond outlines.

Materials

Yardage is based on 42"-wide fabric.

- 1⅜ yards of dark blue print for outer border
- ⅝ yard *each* of 5 different whites and tans for blocks
- ½ yard of red print for inner border
- ⅜ yard *each* of 7 different reds for blocks
- ⅜ yard *each* of 7 different blues for blocks
- ⅜ yard of white print for middle border
- 5¼ yards of fabric for backing
- ¾ yard of blue for binding
- 79" x 94" piece of batting

Cutting

All measurements include ¼" seam allowances.

From each of the 7 reds for blocks, cut:
- 1 strip, 9½" x 42"; crosscut into a total of 20 rectangles, 9½" x 11½"

From each of the 7 blue fabrics, cut:
- 1 strip, 9½" x 42"; crosscut into a total of 20 rectangles, 9½" x 11½"

From each of the 5 white and tan fabrics, cut:
- 2 strips, 8½" x 42"; crosscut into 4 squares, 8½" x 8½", for a total of 40

From the red print for inner border, cut:
- 7 strips, 1¾" x 42"

From the white print for middle border, cut:
- 8 strips, 1¼" x 42"

From the dark blue print, cut:
- 8 strips, 5" x 42"

From the binding fabric, cut:
- 9 strips, 2½" x 42"

Making the Blocks

REFER TO "Making the Crazy Blocks" on pages 10–16 as needed.

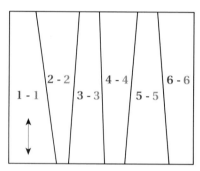

Block Cutting and Sewing Guide
Cut Size: 9½" x 11½"

1. Arrange the 40 red and blue rectangles into five decks of 8 each; each deck should contain eight different fabrics, alternating red and blue. Secure the decks with a pin through all layers until ready to sew.

2. Referring to the block cutting and sewing guide, slice the decks.

3. Shuffle the decks with a traditional shuffle, referring to "Traditional Shuffling" on page 13.

4. Make 40 blocks. Note that the sewing order is the same as the cutting order. Press seam allowances all in one direction. Trim the blocks to 8½" x 8½".

 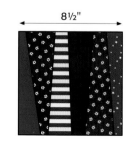

5. Draw a diagonal line from corner to corner in one direction on the back of the white and tan squares. Pair the 40 pieced red and blue blocks right sides together with a white or tan square. Sew ¼" from the drawn line on both sides and press the stitching to set the seam. Use a rotary cutter and ruler to cut each block diagonally on the drawn line to create two blocks. Open the blocks and press the seams toward the white or tan print side. The blocks should measure 8" x 8".

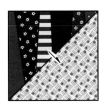

Assembling the Quilt Top

1. Arrange the blocks into 10 horizontal rows of eight blocks each as shown in the quilt diagram. Move and turn the blocks until you're satisfied with the arrangement.

2. Sew the blocks into horizontal rows and press the seams in opposite directions from row to row. Sew the rows together and press the seams in one direction.

3. Sew the inner-border strips together to make one long strip. Refer to "Adding Borders" on page 18. Measure the quilt through the center and cut the inner-border strips to size.

Sew them to the sides of the quilt. Press the seams toward the border strips. Measure and cut the top and bottom inner-border strips and sew them to the quilt.

4. Repeat step 3 for the middle and outer borders.

Finishing Your Quilt

REFER TO "Layering and Basting" on pages 19–21 and "Binding" on pages 21–22.

1. Divide the backing fabric crosswise into two panels, each approximately 94" long. Remove the selvages and sew the pieces together along two long edges to make the backing. Press the seam to one side.

2. Layer the quilt top with the batting and backing, with the backing seam parallel to the sides of the quilt top. Baste the layers together.

3. Hand or machine quilt as desired.

4. Trim the backing and batting even with the quilt top and bind the quilt.

CRAZY CURVY PATCHWORK

With all its crazy curves, this quilt is easy and fun to make. Made up mostly of floral fabric,
it would be great made out of plaids, brights, or seasonal fabrics.

FINISHED QUILT: 55" x 72" • FINISHED BLOCK: 8½" x 8½"

This sweet, curvy Crazy quilt makes up easily with a comfy old-fashioned flair. With a selection of 16 different prints for the blocks, it's a good quilt to help you use up your fabric stash.

Materials

Yardage is based on 42"-wide fabric.

- ⅝ yard of pink print for inner border
- ½ yard *each* of 4 different yellow florals for blocks
- ½ yard *each* of 4 different green florals for blocks
- ½ yard *each* of 4 different pinks for blocks
- ½ yard *each* of 4 different purples for blocks
- 3⅛ yards of fabric for backing
- ⅝ yard of green for binding
- 59" x 76" piece of batting

Fabric Tips

Choose a pink floral fabric featuring medium- to small-scale flowers. Add and subtract additional yellow, purple, and green floral prints in an assortment of medium- and small-scale prints. Once you have your selection, stand back and take a look, using the 10-Foot Rule (page 9).

Cutting

All measurements include ¼" seam allowances.

From each of the 16 fabrics for blocks, cut:
- 1 strip, 12" x 42"; crosscut into 3 squares, 12" x 12", for a total of 48

From the scraps of the green floral, cut:
- 4 squares, 2½" x 2½"

From the pink print, cut:
- 7 strips, 2½" x 42"

From the green fabric, cut:
- 7 strips, 2½" x 42"

Making the Blocks

REFER TO "Making the Crazy Blocks" on pages 10–16 as needed.

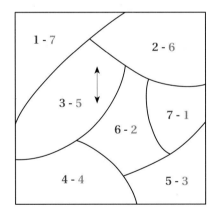

Block Cutting and Sewing Guide
Cut Size: 12" x 12"

1. Arrange the 48 floral squares into six decks of 8 each; each deck should contain eight different fabrics. Secure the decks with a pin through all layers until ready to sew.

2. Referring to the block cutting and sewing guide, slice the decks.

3. Shuffle the decks with a traditional shuffle, referring to "Traditional Shuffling" on page 13.

4. Make 48 blocks. Trim the blocks to 9" x 9".

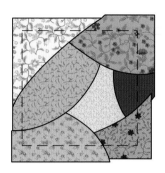 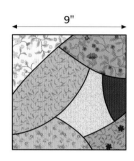

Assembling the Quilt Top

1. Arrange the blocks into six horizontal rows of four blocks each. Move and turn the blocks until you're satisfied with the arrangement. Look through a door peephole or use the 10-foot rule to check the color and block balance.

2. Sew the blocks into horizontal rows and press the seams in opposite directions from row to row. Sew the rows together and press the seams in one direction.

3. Remove the selvages and piece the inner-border strips into one long piece. Press seams in either direction. Cut two 51½" strips for the side borders. Sew them to the sides of the quilt. Press toward the borders.

4. Arrange six blocks on each side of the quilt top for the outer side borders. Sew the blocks together into two vertical rows of six blocks each. Pin and sew the block borders to each side of the quilt top. Press toward the inner border.

5. For the top and bottom borders, cut two inner-border strips 34½" long and eight strips 9" long. Sew a 2½" x 2½" square to each end of each long strip and then add a 2½" x 9" strip to the ends. Press seams away from the square.

6. Pin and sew the pieced border strips to the top and bottom of the quilt. Press seams toward the inner border.

7. For the top and bottom outer border, arrange six blocks across the top and bottom edge of the quilt top. Sew a 2½" x 9" strip to the corner blocks; press toward the inner-border strip. Sew the corner units together with the four middle blocks. Pin and sew the pieced borders to the top and bottom of the quilt. Press seams toward the inner border.

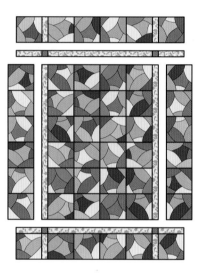

Finishing Your Quilt

Refer to "Layering and Basting" on pages 19–21 and "Binding" on pages 21–22.

1. Divide the backing fabric crosswise into two panels, each approximately 56" long. Remove the selvages and sew the pieces together along two long edges to make the backing. Press the seam to one side.

2. Layer the quilt top with the batting and backing, with the backing seam parallel to the top and bottom of the quilt. Baste the layers together.

3. Hand or machine quilt as desired.

4. Trim the backing and batting even with the quilt top and bind the quilt.

FUNKY CURVY RAIL

This quilt is nothing short of a blast to make. Collect a bunch of green and black prints and go for it. Great for beginners!

FINISHED QUILT: 63" x 80" • FINISHED BLOCK: 8½" x 8½"

*T*he lazy curves in this quilt twine around from block to block, giving it a basket-weave look. The ladybugs crawling across the quilt add a fun splash of color and whimsy. Deviating from the traditional Rail Fence, the curves instead create a funky, curvy rail.

Materials

Yardage is based on 42"-wide fabric.

- 1⅜ yards of green for outer border
- ½ yard of black for inner border
- ⅜ yard *each* of 8 different green prints for blocks
- ⅜ yard *each* of 8 different black-and-white prints for blocks
- ⅛ yard of black for ladybug bodies and heads
- 1 square, 4" x 4", each of 10 different reds for ladybug wings
- 4⅞ yards of fabric for backing
- ¾ yard of fabric for binding
- 69" x 86" piece of batting

Cutting

All measurements include ¼" seam allowances.

From each of the 8 green prints for blocks, cut:

- 1 strip, 10" x 42"; crosscut into 3 rectangles, 10" x 13", for a total of 24

From each of the 8 black-and-white prints, cut:

- 1 strip, 10½" x 42"; crosscut into 3 rectangles, 10" x 13", for a total of 24

From the black fabric, cut:

- 7 strips, 2" x 42"

From the green fabric, cut:

- 8 strips, 5" x 42"

From the binding fabric, cut:

- 8 strips, 2½" x 42"

Fabric Tips

A whimsical selection of fabric sets the scene for this quilt. Choose a range of small-scale green prints combined with small-scale black prints.

Making the Blocks

REFER TO "Making the Crazy Blocks" on pages 10–16 as needed.

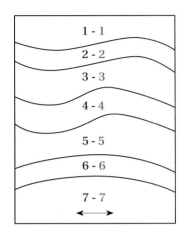

Block Cutting and Sewing Guide
Cut Size: 10" x 13"

1. Arrange the 48 squares into eight decks of 6 each; each deck should contain six different fabrics, alternating green and black. Secure the decks with a pin through all layers until ready to sew.

2. Referring to the block cutting and sewing guide, slice the decks.

3. Shuffle the decks with a traditional shuffle, referring to "Traditional Shuffling" on page 13.

4. Make 48 blocks. Trim the blocks to 9" x 9".

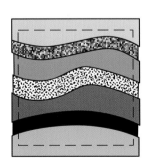
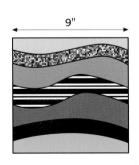

Assembling the Quilt Top

1. Refer to the photograph and quilt diagram to arrange the blocks into eight horizontal rows of six blocks each. Turn the blocks so the lines alternate from vertical to horizontal. Arrange the blocks until you're happy with the setting. Look through a door peephole or use the 10-foot rule to check the color and block balance.

2. Sew the blocks into horizontal rows and press the seams in opposite directions from row to row. Sew the rows together and press the seams in one direction.

3. Sew the inner-border strips together to make one long strip. Refer to "Adding Borders" on page 18. Measure the quilt through the center and cut the inner-border strips to size. Sew them to the sides of the quilt. Press the seams toward the border strips. Measure and cut the top and bottom inner-border strips and sew them to the quilt.

4. Repeat step 3 for the outer border.

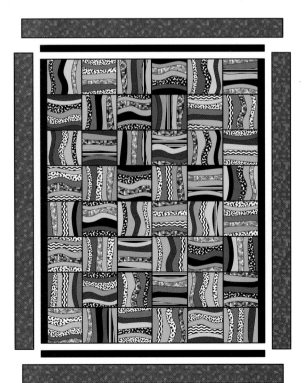

Adding the Appliqués

1. Prepare the ladybug appliqués using the appliqué patterns below and referring to "Fusible-Web Appliqué" on pages 18–19.

2. Referring to the ladybug patterns and the photograph on page 77, position, fuse, and stitch the appliqués in place on the quilt top.

Ace It!

If you want to add spots to your ladybugs, you can machine quilt them with black thread as I did. Or you can fuse circles of black fabric scraps on the wings. I added additional details by stitching around the wings with a machine buttonhole stitch.

Finishing Your Quilt

REFER TO "Layering and Basting" on pages 19–21 and "Binding" on pages 21–22.

1. Divide the backing fabric crosswise into two panels, each approximately 87" long. Remove the selvages and sew the pieces together along two long edges to make the backing. Press the seam to one side.

2. Layer the quilt top with the batting and backing, with the backing seam parallel to the sides of the quilt top. Baste the layers together.

3. Hand or machine quilt as desired.

4. Trim the backing and batting even with the quilt top and bind the quilt.

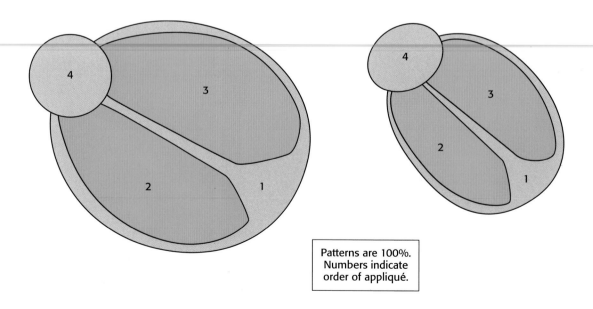

Patterns are 100%.
Numbers indicate
order of appliqué.

THE DAILY GRIND

*You gotta love coffee to make this table runner! Add a few pot holders made
with the appliqués to create the perfect gift for your favorite coffee lover.*
FINISHED QUILT: 15½" x 42½" • FINISHED APPLIQUÉ BLOCK: 8½" x 8½"

Coffee on my mind with its swirling aroma made this table runner a breeze to design. The idea began as a wall hanging; then one night it turned into a hot pad, and finally it percolated into a table runner. All that's missing is the coffee.

Materials

Yardage is based on 42"-wide fabric.

- ⅝ yard of black-and-white print for border blocks
- ½ yard of black for sashing and binding
- ⅜ yard or 1 fat quarter *each* of 4 different background fabrics for coffee cups
- ¼ yard of green print for border blocks
- ¼ yard of plum print for border blocks
- ¼ yard of brown print for border blocks
- 9" x 9" squares of a variety of browns, purples, greens, and blacks for appliqués
- Scraps of red for appliqués
- ¾ yard of fabric for backing
- 20" x 47" piece of batting

Fabric Tips

Choose light, small-scale prints for the coffee cup backgrounds. Warm brown, wine, green, and black colors combine for the pieced border.

Cutting

All measurements include ¼" seam allowances.

From each of the 4 background fabrics, cut:
- 1 square, 9" x 9"

From the black-and-white print, cut
- 3 strips, 5" x 42"; crosscut into 18 squares, 5" x 5"

From each of the green, plum, and brown prints, cut:
- 1 strip, 5" x 42"; crosscut into 6 squares, 5" x 5", for a total of 18 squares

From the black fabric, cut:
- 2 strips, 1" x 42"; crosscut into 5 rectangles, 1" x 9"
- 2 strips, 1" x 37"
- 4 strips, 2½" x 42"

Making the Pieced Blocks

REFER TO "Making the Crazy Blocks" on pages 10–16 as needed.

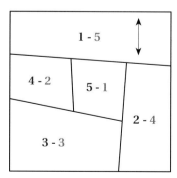

Block Cutting and Sewing Guide
Cut Size: 5" x 5"

1. Arrange the 5" x 5" squares into six decks of six each; each deck should contain six different fabrics, alternating the green, plum, and brown prints with the black-and-white print. Secure the decks with a pin through all layers until ready to sew.

2. Referring to the block cutting and sewing guide, slice the decks.

3. Referring to the shuffling guide, shuffle the decks.

4. Make 36 blocks.

5. For the long side borders, trim 20 of the blocks to 3¼" x 3½" (10 for each side). Trim 6 blocks to 3½" x 3½" (3 for each side).

6. For the short side borders, trim eight of the blocks to 3½" x 3½" (four for each side). Trim two blocks to 3½" x 4" (one for each side).

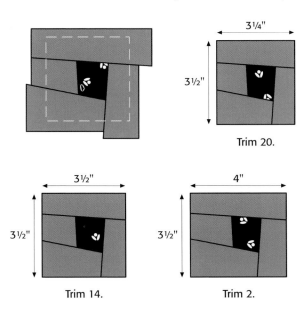

3¼"

3½"

Trim 20.

3½"

3½"

Trim 14.

4"

3½"

Trim 2.

Ace It!

You may want to wait and trim your border blocks after you arrange them around the coffee cup blocks.

Shuffling Guide

USE THE controlled shuffle described on page 14 for the decks in this quilt.

- Remove the top layer of segment 1 and place it on the bottom of the deck.
- Do not shuffle any other segments.

Making the Appliqué Blocks

1. Prepare the appliqués using the appliqué patterns on pages 85–88 and referring to "Fusible-Web Appliqué" on pages 18–19.

2. Refer to the coffee cup patterns and the photograph on page 81 to position, fuse, and stitch the appliqués in place on the background squares.

Assembling the Table Runner

1. Refer to the photograph and arrange the four appliquéd blocks in a row. Turn the blocks so the coffee cups are facing different directions. Sew the blocks together with a 1" x 9" sashing strip between each block. Add a 1" x 9" sashing strip to each end of the blocks. Press seams toward the sashing.

2. Add a 1" x 37" sashing strip to each side of the blocks. Press toward the sashing.

3. Arrange the border blocks around the outside edges of the runner. You will need 10 blocks, 3¼" x 3½", and 3 blocks, 3½" x 3½", for each long side. For each end you will need 4 blocks, 3½" x 3½", and 1 block, 3½" x 4". Once you're satisfied with the layout, sew the pieced border blocks into rows. Press seams in one direction.

4. Add the long side borders to the table runner; press seams toward the sashing. Sew the two remaining borders to the ends of the runner. Press toward the sashing.

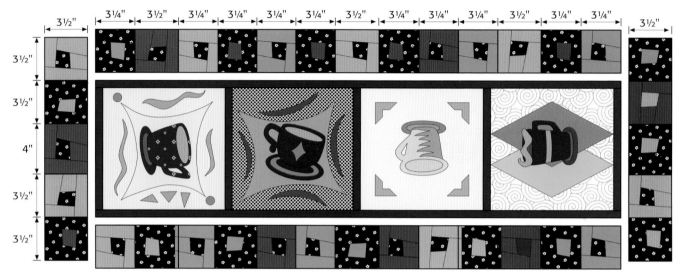

Measurements indicate cut sizes.

Ace It!

If the border is too long, sew the seam allowances a little deeper in a few of the blocks until the border is the correct length.

Finishing Your Quilt

REFER TO "Layering and Basting" on pages 19–21 and "Binding" on pages 21–22.

1. Divide the backing fabric lengthwise into two panels, each approximately 21" x 27". Remove the selvages and sew the pieces together along two short edges to make the backing. Press the seam to one side.

2. Layer the runner with the batting and backing. Baste the layers together.

3. Hand or machine quilt as desired. I machine quilted mine with a random free-motion pattern in the blocks and straight stitching in the sashing and border.

4. Trim the backing and batting even with the quilt top and bind the table runner.

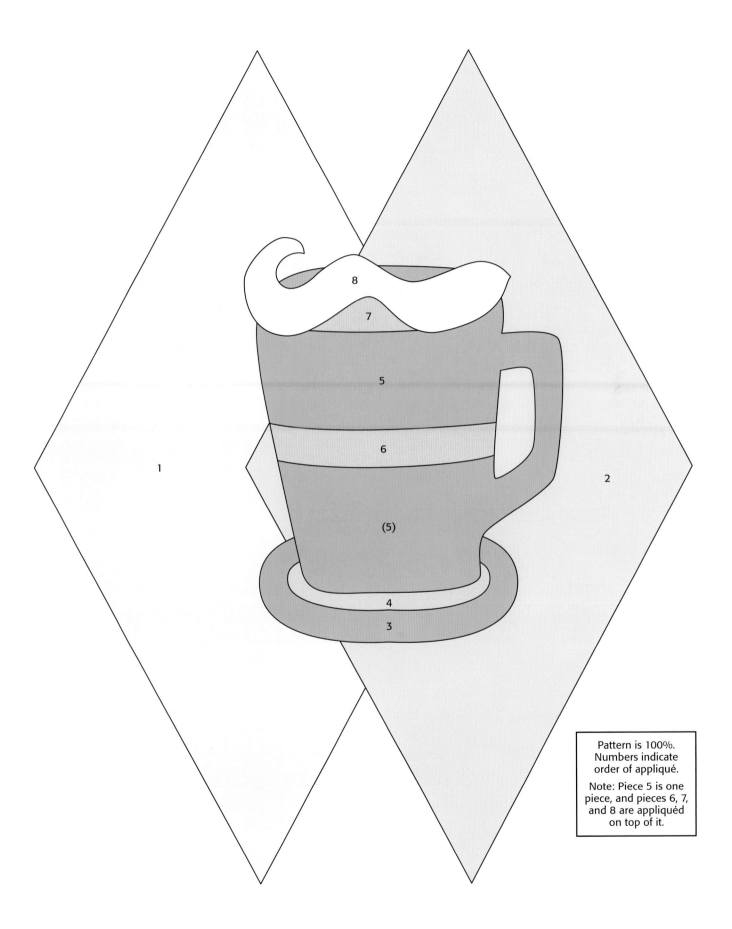

Pattern is 100%.
Numbers indicate
order of appliqué.

Note: Piece 5 is one
piece, and pieces 6, 7,
and 8 are appliquéd
on top of it.

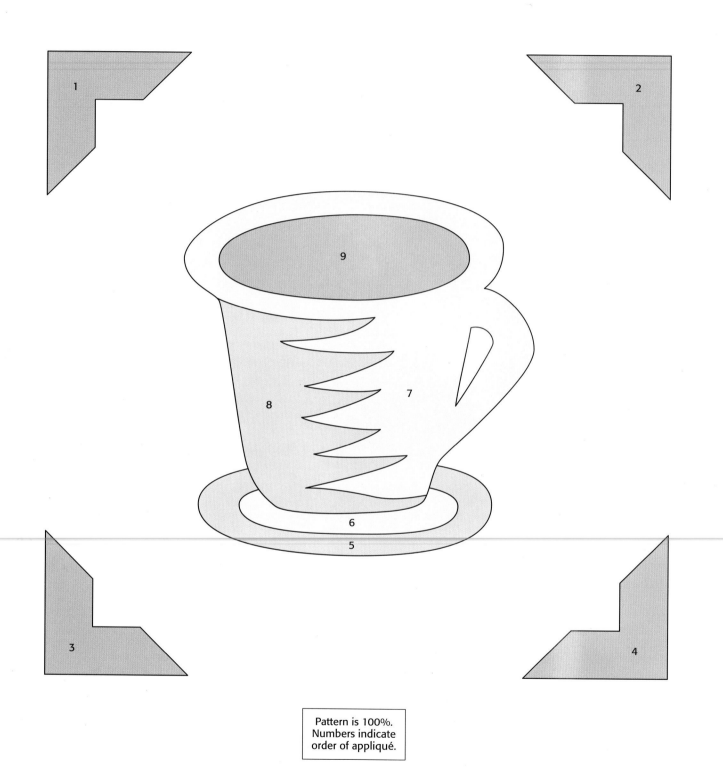

Pattern is 100%.
Numbers indicate
order of appliqué.

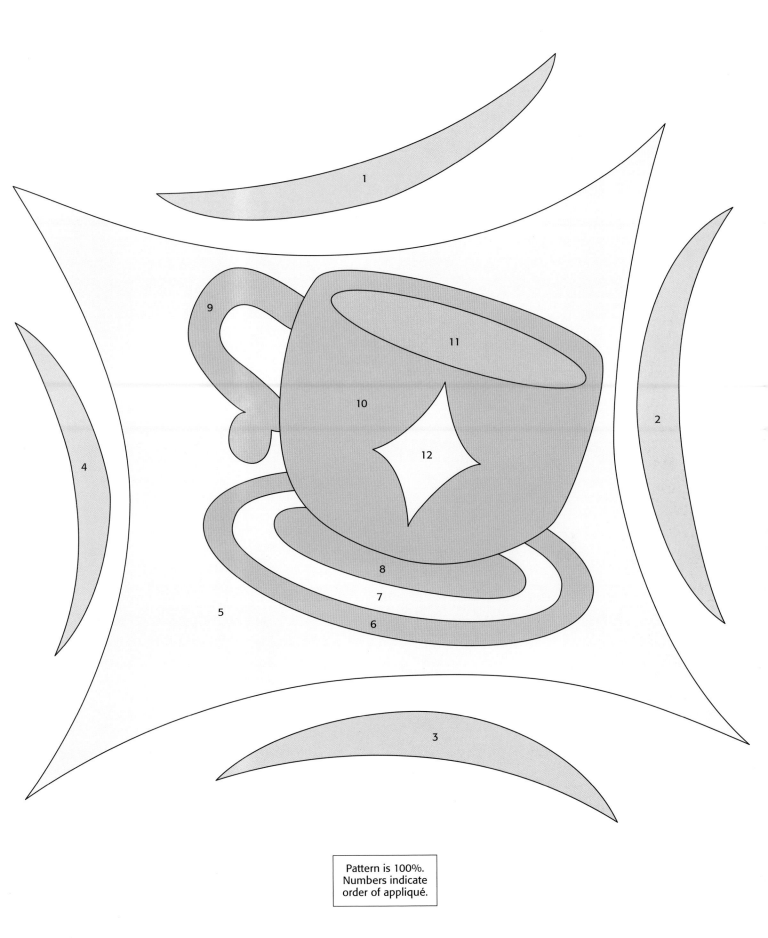

Pattern is 100%.
Numbers indicate
order of appliqué.

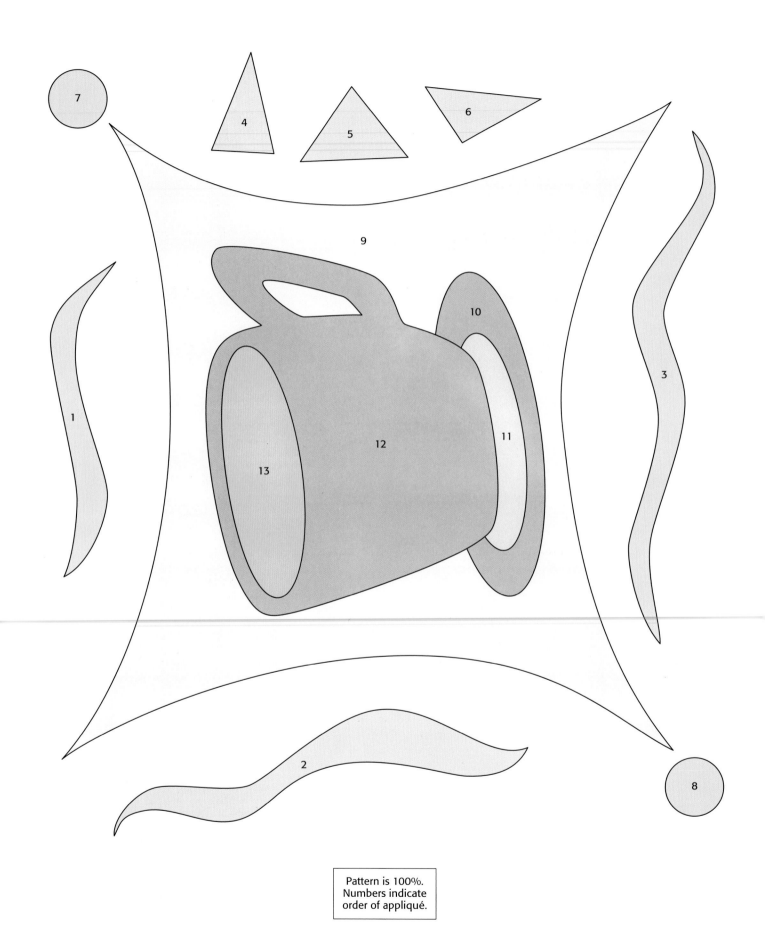

Pattern is 100%.
Numbers indicate
order of appliqué.

TUMBLING TRIANGLES

A great selection of blue and purple batiks make this a dreamy pastel quilt with tumbling triangles.
FINISHED QUILT: 59½" x 75½" • FINISHED BLOCK: 8" x 8"

*L*ight and breezy blue summer skies were the inspiration for this quilt, and of course, batiks were essential! The tumbling triangles are like clouds floating by and the solid blocks give the illusion of breaks in the clouds.

Materials

Yardage is based on 42"-wide fabric.

- 1¼ yards of blue floral batik for outer border
- 1 yard *each* of 5 different light blue batiks for blocks
- 1 yard *each* of 5 different purple and medium blue batiks for blocks
- ⅜ yard of blue batik for inner border
- 4⅝ yards of fabric for backing
- ¾ yard of purple for binding
- 66" x 82" piece of batting

Fabric Tips

Choose a large selection of balmy blue batiks combined with turquoise and purple batiks. Once you have your selection together, stand back and take a look, using the 10-Foot Rule (page 9). No matter what fabrics you choose, make sure your selections contrast with one another.

Cutting

All measurements include ¼" seam allowances.

From each of the 5 light blue batiks, cut:

- 2 strips, 7½" x 42"; crosscut into a total of 38 rectangles, 6" x 7½"
- 1 strip, 6" x 42"; crosscut into a total of 38 rectangles, 4½" x 6"
- 1 square, 8½" x 8½"

From each of the 5 purple and medium blue batiks, cut:

- 2 strips, 7½" x 42"; crosscut into a total of 38 rectangles, 6" x 7½"
- 1 strip, 6" x 42"; crosscut into a total of 38 rectangles, 4½" x 6"
- 1 square, 8½" x 8½"

From the blue batik, cut:

- 6 strips, 1¼" x 42"

From the blue floral batik, cut:

- 7 strips, 5½" x 42"

From the binding fabric, cut:

- 7 strips, 2½" x 42"

Making the Blocks

REFER TO "Making the Crazy Blocks" on pages 10–16 as needed.

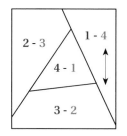

Block Cutting and Sewing Guide
Cut Size: 6" x 7½"

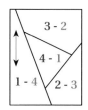

Block Cutting and Sewing Guide
Cut Size: 4½" x 6"

1. Arrange the 38 purple and 38 blue rectangles, 6" x 7½", into 12 decks of six each, and 1 deck of 4. Each deck should contain six different fabrics (four for the deck with just 4 rectangles), alternating the blue with the purple. Secure the decks with a pin through all layers until ready to sew.

2. Repeat step 1 for the 4½" x 6" rectangles.

3. Referring to the block cutting and sewing guides, slice the decks.

4. Referring to the shuffling guide, shuffle the decks.

5. Make 76 large blocks and 76 small blocks. Trim the large blocks to 4½" x 6" and the small ones to 3" x 4½".

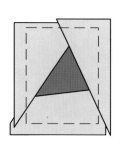
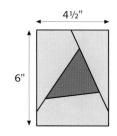

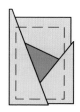
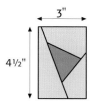

6. Sew 76 small blocks to 76 large blocks, keeping background values the same. Sew the blocks together along the 4½" edges. Press seams toward the large blocks.

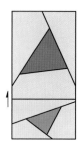

Make 76.

7. Match 38 block sets together, orienting blocks upside down from one another and keeping the background colors the same. Sew the blocks together along the long edge. Press seams in one direction.

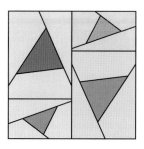

Make 38.

Shuffling Guide

USE THE controlled shuffle described on page 14 for the decks in this quilt.

- Remove the top layer of segment 1 and place it on the bottom of the deck.

- Do not shuffle any other segments.

Assembling the Quilt Top

1. Arrange the pieced blocks and the 8½" squares into eight rows of six blocks each. Move and turn the blocks until you're satisfied with the arrangement. Look through a door peephole or use the 10-foot rule to check the color and block balance.

2. Sew the blocks into horizontal rows and press the seams in opposite directions from row to row. Sew the rows together and press the seams in one direction.

3. Sew the inner-border strips together to make one long strip. Refer to "Adding Borders" on page 18. Measure the quilt through the center and cut the inner-border strips to size. Sew them to the sides of the quilt. Press the seams toward the border strips. Measure and cut the top and bottom inner-border strips and sew them to the quilt.

4. Repeat step 3 for the outer border.

Finishing Your Quilt

REFER TO "Layering and Basting" on pages 19–21 and "Binding" on pages 21–22.

1. Divide the backing fabric crosswise into two panels, each approximately 83" long. Remove the selvages and sew the pieces together along two long edges to make the backing. Press the seam to one side.

2. Layer the quilt top with the batting and backing, with the backing seam parallel to the sides of the quilt top. Baste the layers together.

3. Hand or machine quilt as desired.

4. Trim the backing and batting even with the quilt top and bind the quilt.

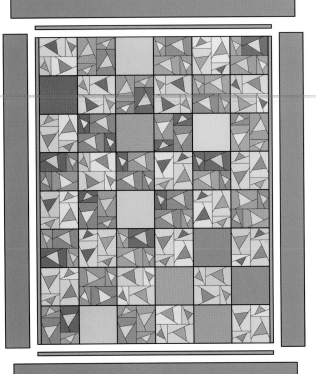

LOUNGE LIZARDS

The vibrant colors and wacky triangles suggest excitement and energy, counterbalanced by reptiles that seem to represent the slow, steady passage of time.

FINISHED QUILT: 43½" x 67" • FINISHED BLOCK: 6½" x 7"

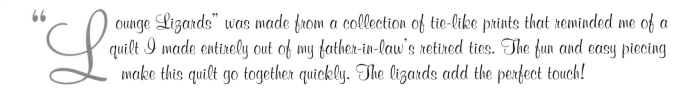

"*Lounge Lizards*" was made from a collection of tie-like prints that reminded me of a quilt I made entirely out of my father-in-law's retired ties. The fun and easy piecing make this quilt go together quickly. The lizards add the perfect touch!

Materials

Yardage is based on 42"-wide fabric.

- 1 yard of red print for outer border
- ⅜ yard *each* of 5 different black prints for blocks (or 20 assorted black squares, 8½" x 8½")
- ⅜ yard *each* of 5 different bright-colored prints for blocks (or 20 assorted bright-colored squares, 8½" x 8½")
- ⅜ yard of black for inner border
- 1 square, 10" x 10", *each* of 3 greens, 1 brown, and 1 black for lizard appliqués
- 2¾ yards of fabric for backing
- ⅝ yard of black for binding
- 48" x 71" piece of batting

Cutting

All measurements include ¼" seam allowances.

From the 5 black prints, cut:
- 20 squares, 8½" x 8½"

From the 5 bright-colored prints, cut:
- 20 squares, 8½" x 8½"

From the black fabric, cut:
- 5 strips, 1½" x 42"

From the red fabric, cut:
- 6 strips, 5" x 42"

From the binding fabric, cut:
- 6 strips, 2½" x 42"

Making the Blocks

REFER TO "Making the Crazy Blocks" on pages 10–16.

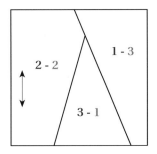

Block Cutting and Sewing Guide
Cut Size: 8½" x 8½"

1. Arrange the 20 black print squares with the 20 bright-colored print squares into 10 decks of 4 each. Each deck should contain four different fabrics, alternating the black with a bright. Secure the decks with a pin through all layers until ready to sew.

2. Referring to the block cutting and sewing guide, slice the decks. Vary the cutting from deck to deck as I did so that some of the triangles are taller and some are shorter.

3. Referring to the shuffling guide, shuffle the decks.

4. Make 40 blocks. Trim the blocks to 7" x 7½".

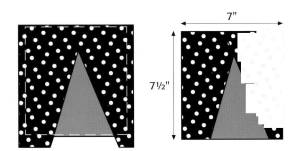

Shuffling Guide

Use the controlled shuffle described on page 14 for the decks in this quilt.

- Remove the top layer of segment 1 and place it on the bottom of the deck.
- Do not shuffle any other segments.

Assembling the Quilt Top

1. Refer to the photograph on page 93. Arrange the blocks into eight horizontal rows of five blocks each. Move and turn the blocks until you're satisfied with the arrangement. Look through a door peephole or use the 10-foot rule to check the color and block balance.

2. Sew the blocks into horizontal rows and press the seams in opposite directions from row to row. Sew the rows together and press the seams in one direction.

3. Sew the inner-border strips together to make one long strip. Refer to "Adding Borders" on page 18. Measure the quilt through the center and cut the inner-border strips to size. Sew them to the sides of the quilt. Press the seams toward the border strips. Measure and cut the top and bottom inner-border strips and sew them to the quilt. Repeat for the outer border.

Adding the Appliqués

1. Enlarge the appliqué patterns. Referring to "Fusible-Web Appliqué" on pages 18–19, prepare the appliqué shapes.

2. Referring to the photograph on page 93, position, fuse, and stitch the appliqués in place on the quilt top.

Finishing Your Quilt

Refer to "Layering and Basting" on pages 19–21 and "Binding" on pages 21–22.

1. Divide the backing fabric crosswise into two panels, each approximately 49" long. Remove the selvages and sew the pieces together along two long edges to make the backing. Press the seam to one side.

2. Layer the quilt top with the batting and backing, with the backing seam parallel to the top and bottom of the quilt. Baste the layers together.

3. Hand or machine quilt as desired.

4. Trim the backing and batting even with the quilt top and bind the quilt.

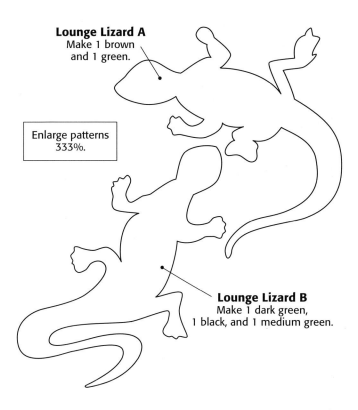

Lounge Lizard A
Make 1 brown and 1 green.

Enlarge patterns 333%.

Lounge Lizard B
Make 1 dark green, 1 black, and 1 medium green.

ABOUT THE AUTHOR

Ever since she was a young girl, Karla Alexander enjoyed pinning and arranging fabric scraps together. As a teenager, the gift of a quilt sparked her appreciation of the art of quiltmaking. Years later, while living in Kodiak, Alaska, Karla faced the challenge of dark, rainy winters and long summer days by exploring quiltmaking. Now, her pastime has grown into a passion for the endless possibilities of quilting.

Since 1997, Karla has taught quilt classes and designed quilts. Under the name Saginaw Street Quilt Company, she has created and released her own line of patterns. She has been a featured teacher at many quilt retreats and has taught more than four thousand students how to make quilts using her stacking methods. She has made well over two hundred quilts with hundreds more waiting to be made.

Karla now lives in beautiful Salem, Oregon, with her husband, Don, and youngest son, William. Her oldest son, Shane, lives in Idaho, and her second son, Kelly, is enlisted in the navy. Karla currently teaches and works at Greenbaum's Quilted Forest in Salem and takes great pleasure in sharing her love of quiltmaking and inspiring quiltmakers of all ages and skill levels.